MEMOIRS

OF A

BUTTERFLY

A STORY OF METAMORPHOSIS

LINDA LAYTON PAOLONE

ISBN 978-1688096363

PREFACE

Everyone has a story. If everyone wrote their memoirs down on paper for others to read there would probably be many interesting stories. But most people don't. So why should I write mine? My story is probably not so different from others. Some people have had easier, more privileged lives than mine. Some have had it far more difficult.

But for some reason, it has been on my mind for a long time to document my story. Maybe it is an innate desire for your people to really know you, to understand who you truly are. Maybe it is the common human desire to leave a mark on history. Most people live their lives and then die. After a generation or two, they are forgotten unless they happen to be famous. Most people don't know much at all of what their parents or grandparents experienced in their lives. They don't have any idea what it was like to live in their day and age.

As I write this book my granddaughters, Avery and Madison, are four years old. I have spent three days a week with them practically from the day they were born. If something happened to me right now they would probably remember some things about me, but not much. I would like them to know me, another good reason to write my memoirs.

Then again maybe no one really cares. Most people are only concerned about their own lives and meeting their own needs. We are a self-absorbed, self-centered people after all. And as to everything else... well, it is what it is.

So maybe the real reason to write it all down is simply to try and make some sense of it all. How did you become the person you are? Why did you make the choices you made in this journey? Why do you feel the way you feel about certain things? Does it matter? Or should you just let it be... 'It is what it is'. Just finish your time and move on to whatever lies ahead.

In my case, I'm not sure I have wanted to share the most intimate and darkest parts of my life. I haven't shared it with many people and don't know if I want to now either. But the bottom line is that I believe God wanted me to do this. So what other people think of it is not the most important thing.

I wrote the childhood portion of Part 1, "Life As A Caterpillar", which is mostly a compilation of random memories, from a child's perspective, and in the third person. It seemed like it might be easier to write it that way, detached somehow. And I realized why I had put this off for so long. Something inside just hurts when you remember certain things. And who wants to do that? It is like when you hear an old song and you can remember exactly where you were and what you were doing when the song was popular. You can feel exactly what you felt at that time. It's hard work. It is so much easier to walk through life with a hardened heart. Just don't feel anything, ok? But, is it really easier in the long run? Anyway, the childhood memories are random but they do lay the foundation for what is to come. I also found it interesting how much I don't remember about my childhood.

As I continued to write I realized that to write in such a detached manner did not produce a very interesting result. History without heart is boring, just facts, monotone. A still, small voice kept asking me, "Yes, but how did you feel about that?" and saying, "No, you are not done yet. Delve deeper."

Some of this story is just downright depressing. So the challenge became: to write the story without getting bogged down in a full-time pity party. We don't want to walk around with a victim mentality, do we? We don't want to become completely self-absorbed. So where is the balance? Some days I just felt raw! So I would take a break for a few days and try to get back in touch with the hope that lives within me. All the things that hurt me just became part of the story. And there is light at the end of the tunnel.

And another thing, how do you tell the truth about things that happened without throwing anyone else under the bus? Again, it's a fine balance. In any event, everyone has their issues and their reasons for doing what they do. Love covers a multitude of sins. I have made many poor choices in my life (Proverbs says even a child is known by his deeds). I have hurt others in the process. So I have tried and am still doing my best to forgive all who hurt me as I also need forgiveness from those that I have hurt. If anyone ever reads these memoirs please view them with that in mind.

Note to any of my Buddhist friends, if any of you ever read this: you may be offended by my description of the practice of Buddhism. It is written from my perspective, based on my own experience. I spoke my truth without bothering to be politically correct. This was not, however, meant to demean any particular person. I had many dear friends in the Buddhist organization, people I love still. Some of those were even my senior leaders. I would ask, as my first husband, Rick, once asked me, "Please read it to the end."

And, to my children, some of what I have written about your father may be difficult for you to read. I have always tried my best to protect you and allow you to just love your dad, so I have not shared much. However, this story is about how our relationship impacted me. This is my history. I want to tell the truth. Some things I will never share since I do believe that some things between a man and a woman should remain private, even if they don't stay together. In any event, please remember that your dad had many good points, as well as the bad. He tried his best to help many people, in the way he thought best. And many people loved him. And he loved you both! And after all, we are all imperfect human beings, aren't we?

Not everything in my story was dark and dreary. I gave birth to two amazing children! I am so proud of how they have grown as human beings. I have two beautiful granddaughters who bring me such joy. I have had the opportunity to go to many places that I never imagined I would see. I have met many amazing people. I accomplished things I would not have thought possible. And most important, I encountered God and found hope, which is the real story.

So I have decided to just write. No matter how I feel. No matter what anyone else thinks, and we will see where it goes. Maybe I will do something with this when I'm finished, maybe I won't. Maybe others will read it, maybe they won't. Maybe it will end up in the trashcan. But I will make those decisions later. For now, I will just write and remember.

MEMOIRS OF A BUTTERFLY

Butterfly: Someone seen as not serious; someone flighty and unreliable. (Wiktionary)

Butterfly: A person chiefly occupied with the pursuit of pleasure. (Merriam-Webster)

Butterfly: A creature that looks like a worm, crawls on the ground and then goes through a metamorphosis. It actually liquefies in the cocoon, becoming a new and different creature. The new creature is delicate but resilient. And it can fly, flitting from flower to flower, tasting the nectar of life. Perhaps butterflies are angels in disguise. (Linda)

I

LIFE AS A CATERPILLAR

1

Linda Marie Layton entered this world on March 14, 1947, in Tacoma, Washington. Her mother almost miscarried when she was three months pregnant. Mommy said Daddy pushed her down the stairs. They gave Mommy a drug, DES, to keep her from having a miscarriage. Years later they discovered the drug could cause Linda problems later on in life but the drug worked. Linda hung in there.

Linda arrived with long, curly, black hair, which made Mommy think Linda wasn't her baby. Mommy told the nurses so, insisting someone switched babies. She wanted her own baby back! Linda was a sickly child and almost didn't make it. An obstruction in her stomach prevented her from digesting her milk. It came back up and choked her. If she had been a boy, the condition would have required surgery, but the doctors said girls normally outgrow this issue.

Linda's parents slept with the light on for the first three months of her life, keeping a watchful eye. Her mother later told her that on one occasion she ran for a doctor in the middle of the night while Daddy held Linda upside-side-down by her feet, swatting her bottom to get her to breathe. She was turning blue. Mommy said she didn't know if her baby girl would be alive when she got back. Life began with a struggle, but Linda survived.

Linda's older brother, Larry was five years old when she was born. He wasn't thrilled to have a baby sister. Mommy said Larry became so upset he broke out in a rash and had to go to the hospital. She said she couldn't leave baby Linda alone with Larry. She never explained why. Although, Mommy said Larry got mad one day at his grandfather, Didi, because he was lying on the couch on top of one of Larry's toy cars. Mommy said Larry got so mad at Didi he hit him with a broomstick. Perhaps there was a good reason Mommy didn't want to leave Linda alone with Larry. But Mommy said a lot of things. Anyway, as they grew older, Larry turned out to be a great brother to Linda.

And kids will be kids, for goodness sake. At five years of age, God blessed Linda with a younger brother, Stevie. Linda used to hear her mother comment all the time as she changed Stevie's diaper, "Keep that thing down or I'll put pepper on it." Linda wondered what would happen if Mommy put pepper on it. Maybe it would do some kind of trick or something. So one day, Mommy left baby Stevie alone with Linda and she found out. That pepper must have burned like fire because poor little Stevie cried and cried. Yes, kids will be kids. They probably should not be watching babies.

Linda's earliest memories are vague, such as the time she ran down the street hysterical over something. What was she running from? She doesn't recall. She also remembers the Christmas party when everyone got drunk and someone knocked over the Christmas tree. Vague memories. Linda's family drank a bit.

Her first vivid memory occurred when she was five years old, as she sat on the kitchen counter at Nana's house, crying. Her parents were leaving for someplace called California. She and Larry had to stay with Nana, Didi and Uncle Ralph. Her parents would send for them when they could. Linda loved her grandparents, as most little girls do, but she couldn't understand why her parents were leaving her. She thought, *"Why aren't they taking me with them? Are they ever really going to come back and get me?"* Many years later Mommy told her they had to leave in a hurry because some drug dealers were after Daddy. But then, Mommy said a lot of things.

Life with Nana and Didi was fun for Linda. Nana would let her make egg salad sandwiches with the egg slicer. She always left some hard-boiled eggs for her in the fridge when she left for work in the morning. Only Nana worked because both Didi and Uncle Ralph were crippled. They suffered from Muscular Dystrophy or Muscular Atrophy, or possibly one of each. Anyway, they both had a hard time walking and Didi's hands were weak. It was hard for him to lift his mug of beer or even smoke his Old Gold cigarettes. He had to use one hand to help the other get up to his mouth.

Didi let Linda cut paper dolls out of the Sears and Roebuck catalog. When she finished, he told her, "Linda, pick up all those itsy-bitsy, teensy-weensy pieces of paper you left all over the floor." He didn't get mad though. He was always sweet. Didi also let Linda shave with a real razor (without the blade, of course) and his shaving cup and brush. He taught her how to smear cream all over her face with the brush and then take it off with the razor. She loved that!

Nana also gave Linda an old flour sifter. One of her favorite things to do was sit with a big pile of dirt and sift and sift and sift until that dirt was as fine as could be. That was much more fun than playing with dolls.

Linda spent a lot of time listening to records on her little record player. She already showed a great love of music, especially sad songs. Her favorite song? "The Little White Cloud That Cried" by Johnny Ray.

Nana wrote lots of letters to Mommy after they moved to California. Linda got to read them many years later, after Nana died. She always told Mommy we were doing okay but Larry and Linda did fight a lot. On several occasions she reported, " Linda has been eating the dog food again."

Eventually, Linda's parents got settled in California and sent money to Nana to bring Larry and Linda down there on the train. How exciting! Linda got to climb up on the top bunk in the sleeper car. She saw some pretty steep mountains out the window of the train too, which was kind of scary. The best part of the trip was finally getting to California and seeing her Mommy and Daddy again. How long had it been since they left, six months, nine months, or a year? It seemed like forever to a little girl. Little did she know, this would be the first of many moves she would make and many places she would see in her life. She would also have many names.

Mommy and Daddy rented a duplex in Baldwin Hills, and then two other places. Linda doesn't remember much about those places but Mommy did get a belly on her then. Stevie was on the way. Not long after, they rented a place in Huntington Park. Linda remembers that place because it was perched on a high hill, and had 93 steps to climb up to the house. She started kindergarten and it was Larry's job to walk home from school with her. Larry didn't like his job much and therefore didn't take it too seriously. Every day became an adventure as she would end up standing alone at the bottom of those stairs, trying to get up her courage to run as fast as she could to the top. You see there were lots of bushes with lots of bees on the way up the hill. There were also tarantulas in the backyard. One more thing, Larry kept a big turtle in a pen up behind the house. He warned Linda she should never touch the turtle on its neck because her finger would get stuck between the neck and the shell and would not come out until there was a thunderstorm. Linda smiled to herself the day the turtle ran, well, crawled away. Funny, the things kids remember, usually the bad things.

One cool thing happened at that house though. Mommy and Daddy bought their very first television, a black and white with tubes in the back, which Daddy had to replace all the time. Linda liked to go with Daddy to the store to use their tube-testing machine. Daddy had to take all the tubes with him and test them all to find the bad one. There were so many really fun shows to watch: Walt Disney World, Romper Room, Engineer Bill, Cecil and Beanie, Howdy Doody and Clarabelle the Clown. Linda loved the television.

The family liked to go to the beach after Daddy came home from work. Linda could always smell the fishy smell of the ocean before she could even see the water. She loved the ocean! Even after Mommy pulled her out of a riptide, she had no fear of the water. She didn't like to be in the sun though. If Mommy made her stay on the blanket, she would cover herself with towels so her skin wouldn't get a tan. She thought a suntan would make her look dirty.

Nana, Didi and Uncle Ralph moved to California and rented a place in Hollywood, near Santa Monica Blvd and Western. It was a tiny little house behind a store. Linda spent most Sunday nights with her family over at Nana's house. Mommy complained about it though. She said Nana would get mad if they didn't go and she didn't want to go every Sunday. They usually drank lots of beer on those Sundays. The family sat together and played Canasta sometimes. That was lots of fun. Nana always played Lawrence Welk on the TV. Sometimes there were fights too. Mommy got mean when she was drunk. Nana too. Linda tried to stay out of the way on those nights. She tried to be invisible.

One night, as the family sat around the dining room table, Daddy pretended to put voodoo curses on people. He pounded on the table as if it were a drum. He was joking, of course. Then Daddy did something that made Linda mad at him. So in her mind, she pretended to put a curse on Daddy. She thought, *"I hope you burn yourself with your cigarette."* That night Daddy fell asleep with a cigarette in his hand and caught the bed on fire. Scary! *"Did I make that happen? I will never do that again!"* Daddy didn't get hurt, thank God!

Another night on the way home from Nana's house, one of those nights when everyone drank too much beer, Mommy and Daddy started fighting. Mommy yelled at Daddy and all of a sudden she raised a beer bottle in the air to hit him. This scared Linda because Daddy was driving the car. Linda screamed, "Stop it! You're going to get us all killed!" Amazingly, Mommy stopped. She put the bottle down and stayed quiet the rest of the way home. This was one of the few times Linda ever said anything like that to her Mommy.

Nana loved little Linda and always treated her well, but a couple of things happened at Nana's house that Linda held in her heart against her Nana. One night, Nana got drunk and when Didi got up to go to the bathroom, Nana walked behind him, hunched over, shuffling along, and mocking him. Linda's heart broke for her Didi.

Nana had a boyfriend for a while. Stanley came to Nana's house and Linda saw them sitting on the porch swing in the backyard together. Poor Didi. How sad it must have made him.

Maybe that's why years later, when Linda got the phone call informing her that Didi died, she responded, "I'll bet she's happy now!" People sometimes react in strange ways when someone dies.

When Linda was seven years old, Mommy and Daddy moved to Lakeview Terrace, up near Hansen Dam. Linda got to take the school bus to school. She started making some new friends. Her school, Stonehurst Elementary, had stones all over the front of it. Linda gained a little more freedom in her life, being able to take the bus. She could also skate outside now, all by herself. She joined the Bluebirds, an organization similar to Girl Scouts, and Mommy drove her to the meetings up in Kagel Canyon. This was a happy time. Mommy took her to a little church up there. They let Linda get baptized. Mommy even sent her to Vacation Bible School that summer. Linda studied hard to learn her Bible verses in VBS and came in second place in their contest. She got to choose her prize and since she already owned a Bible, she chose a framed picture of Jesus. At a ceremony at the church on a Sunday night, she got to go up to the front of the church to receive her prize. She beamed with pride! However, after she returned to her metal folding chair, she stood to sing a hymn and put the picture down on the chair. It slid right off the chair and fell on the floor. The glass broke diagonally from top to bottom. Linda couldn't believe it! She worked so hard for that picture. What hurt her the most? No one ever bothered to fix the picture for her. She finally figured none of that stuff must have been very important after all.

That broken picture may have been a sign of bad times to come. Mommy and Daddy stopped going to church. The liquor started to flow in Linda's house. Various relatives came from Georgia to visit and it seemed they all drank a lot. Daddy was the seventh son of the seventh son, which is supposed to mean something important. All of his brothers who came to visit were drunks. Uncle Hugh liked to hide rubbing alcohol behind the toilet. And you had to watch out for Uncle Larry. When drunk, he liked to give wet sloppy kisses. Linda liked Uncle Roy, but he was a drunk too. Daddy had a nephew named Arthur. He came to the house with his wife Janet a lot. One night they had a big fight and somehow Janet got stuck trying to crawl out the bathroom window. The next thing Mommy knew, the police were hauling Daddy away in a police car. She got upset and started yelling at the police, "He didn't do anything, he was sleeping!" Such a crazy night!

Many nights Linda woke up hearing drunken fights. For example, one night she heard Mommy screaming, "He's killing me! Help! He's killing me!" Linda ran to the kitchen only to find her mother standing holding a butcher knife in her hand, threatening Daddy. *What are you doing, Mommy?* Mommy used to say Daddy would hit her where it wouldn't show. It is possible, I guess, but then Mommy said a lot of things.

One night Linda overheard Mommy accusing Daddy of doing something wrong with a lady, Vivian. Vivian lived nearby with "her three brats" as Mommy called them. Vivian didn't have a husband. Linda didn't understand what Mommy thought he did wrong. Besides, Mommy said a lot of things.

Larry and Linda did their fair share of fighting too. One day they were home alone. For some reason, Larry chased after Linda with a croquet mallet in his hand. She ran toward the front door and made the mistake of turning around to see if Larry was still coming after her. As she turned, the croquet mallet came sailing through the air, right across the room and hit her in the eye. She got a horrible black eye, which lasted for two weeks. And she had a bone in her nose that hurt for months. It didn't seem like Larry ever even got in trouble for hurting her either!

Linda remembers some good things too, not just the bad things all the time. Mommy sometimes took her to Hansen Dam to swim. They lived too far away from the ocean now to go there but at least she still got to swim. She loved being in the water. Her new favorite song was "**Don't Be Cruel**" by Elvis Presley. Arthur and Janet bought the record for her. She got so excited when they pulled up in front of her house to bring it to her, she ran out of the house as fast as she could and slipped on the wet sidewalk. She hit her bottom hard and boy did it hurt! That's okay though. She still loved the record and played it all the time. Mommy and Daddy raised Linda on country music. Elvis sparked her love for rock-and-roll.

Linda made friends with a girl who lived up the street, named Margaret. Her mommy made homemade tortillas and beans. Sometimes Margaret's mommy offered some to Linda. Oh, how she loved that! Mommy wasn't happy when Linda wouldn't eat her dinner that night, saying, "Linda, you have been up there eating that raw dough again, haven't you?" Linda didn't care. She could eat that "raw dough" every night. It tasted delicious! Mommy didn't cook very much anyway. Linda ate a lot of TV dinners so those homemade beans and tortillas were a real treat!

Mommy and Daddy liked to go camping, which Linda loved. Once, they camped at Sweet Water Lake in Agua Dulce. Walt Disney filmed the Spin and Marty series there. There was a big pond used for breeding bullfrogs. There were big signs everywhere saying, "Do not catch the frogs." But Linda woke up one morning, to see Daddy frying up frog legs over the fire. She wondered why Daddy didn't obey the signs but she decided to try the frog legs anyway. Delicious! They tasted just like chicken!

Linda also got her first and only swim lesson there. Daddy put her on his shoulders and then threw her off into the lake. That's okay, she still loved the water, but she never became a very good swimmer.

The family also camped at Kern River once. At least their trip started at Kern River. While Daddy and Larry were off fishing, Mommy saw some rats and freaked out. When the men returned Mommy insisted they leave, so they had to pack up the whole camp. Linda got mad because she thought they were going home. Daddy saved the day though. He found another place they could go, not as nice but better than going home.

The house on Osborne and Kismet in Lakeview Terrace is gone now. The State of California took it by eminent domain and it became the Osborne onramp of the 210 Freeway.

4.

Next stop… Sylmar. Mommy and Daddy rented a nice house on Lyle Street across from the Country Cousins Market. Daddy put a swirly finish on the ceiling of the house that was so pretty. And a nice girl lived next door named Carlotta. Her parents took Linda to church with them a couple of times. She liked that. Linda also loved playing Jacks and Pickup Sticks with Carlotta.

There were still a lot of orchards around Sylmar in those days, mostly olive trees. There was also a girl's reform school nearby with big gray concrete walls so high you couldn't see inside. Years later Linda heard that the daughter of a famous actress, Lana Turner, was in there because she killed her mother's boyfriend. One day, as Linda played with some friends in the olive grove next to the reform school, she heard some girls talking on the other side of the wall. They yelled to her, "Do you have any cigarettes?" Linda laughed and said, "No, I am only nine and I don't smoke yet." But Linda thought to herself, "*That place is where the bad girls go. I will probably go there someday.*" She wondered many times, later in her life, why she would think such a thing. Why would she believe she was bad?

Linda was fascinated with those gray walls because they had all kinds of writing on them. Kids would use the olives that fell from the trees to write on the walls. One day she left school early because she didn't feel well. Apparently, they let kids walk home alone in those days because alone she was. Or did Linda get upset about something and leave the school ground without permission? Who knows? Anyway, passing by those walls, she couldn't resist. She picked up an olive and wrote the 'F' word. Afterward, she was sorry about it and hoped nobody saw her do it. She decided she didn't want to do that again. She felt guilty.

One bad thing happened at the pretty Lyle house… Daddy got sick. They said he had something called tuberculosis and had to go into the hospital. So Mommy had to go to work and they couldn't stay at the Lyle house anymore. The kids moved with Mommy to a tiny little house on Dyer Street. Linda had to share a room with both of her brothers. There was a nice little hill in front of the house though, which Linda liked to roll down.

The VA hospital would not allow Linda to go inside Daddy's room. She couldn't even go inside the building. A couple of times Mommy took her and let her stand on the ground below, under Daddy's window. He would come to the window and wave at her. Linda waved and waved. She really missed him. Daddy used to do funny things like pretending to pull a coin out of her ear. He would also pretend to pull a hair out of her head, make it stiff with a little spit and then balance it on his finger. Linda knew Daddy loved her. How long did he stay in the hospital? Was it six months, nine months or a year? Linda didn't understand the passage of time very well yet. Anyway, Daddy's treatment must not have worked because he ended up having surgery and they took out three-quarters of one lung.

Linda got sick a lot at the Dyer house. She got colds and the flu and had to go get penicillin shots from Dr. "D". He would always tell her to come back in three or four days, which always meant she would have to get another shot. Once, Linda and both of her brothers got Scarletina (Scarlet Fever), all at the same time. No fun. Neither was Whooping Cough.

Linda learned that you couldn't talk to Mommy about personal things. She noticed some changes were happening in her body and wanted to tell Mommy. She found Mommy in the bathroom where she put on her make-up, getting ready for work. Excited, she said, "Look Mommy, peach fuzz!" But Mommy didn't like that. She turned around and glared at Linda and told her, "Get out of here, Linda!" So she did. She was confused though, she didn't understand what she had done wrong. Was that dirty? *"Maybe Mommy just doesn't like me."*

5.

Mommy must have started making more money at some point because she and the kids moved again, this time to a bigger house by the railroad tracks in Sylmar. Linda didn't have to share a room with her brothers anymore. Mommy wasn't home much though so Larry had to watch her all the time. He must not have liked that because he got mad at her a lot. One time he wrestled with her and got a little rough. Linda told Mommy about it and Mommy told her. "If it happens again, just go tell the neighbors." Again, it seemed like Mommy didn't do anything about it. Linda doesn't remember ever having a real babysitter. Larry may have been tired of having to watch her and little Stevie. A girl lived down the street named Dottie. Larry seemed to like her, so he probably would rather have been with her.

Some kids in the neighborhood liked to go down to the railroad tracks and watch the trains go by. Sometimes there were open cars and you could see hobos sitting inside. One day, the kids were having a great time throwing rocks at the hobos. Stevie got upset because he thought they were going to hurt someone. Sweet Stevie. It's amazing the things kids will think of to do when left unsupervised.

Years later, Larry told Linda that Mommy used to bring men home a lot. He said they tried to butter him up, but he wasn't going for it. Funny, the only men Linda remembers coming there were boyfriends to each other. They all rode to Disneyland together in a convertible, with the top down. One guy drove and the other sat in the passenger seat with his feet up on the dashboard. Everyone laughed and had a good time. Favorite song: "**Angel Baby**" by Rosie and the Originals.

6.

When Daddy got out of the hospital, the family moved to Arleta, on Fillmore Street. This house sat across the street from a big flood control district, also known as "the wash". Linda made some new friends and they liked to go play in the wash.

Linda was twelve years old now and attended Junior High School. Mom drank a lot more these days and Linda never knew what condition Mom would be in when she got home from school. Her drink of choice these days was Jim Beam instead of beer.

One day, Linda came home upset because her sewing teacher gave her a failing grade on her first sewing project, a gym bag. She claimed Linda had cheated by taking her project home. Only Linda didn't know she wasn't allowed to do that. She didn't mean to cheat. She never received a failing grade before. Unfortunately, Mom was very drunk when Linda got home. Mom decided to call the school and complain about the teacher! Linda felt humiliated. It was so embarrassing to have a mother who was drunk all the time! You never wanted any of your friends to come to your house. And now the whole school would know about her too. Linda ran out the front door and started walking. She kept walking until about 8:00 that night. Since she changed into shorts when she got home from school, she got pretty cold after it got dark. She had nowhere to go. She had no choice so she turned around and walked back home.

Upon Linda's return, the police came to the house. They came into her bedroom to talk to her. The policeman asked her, "Is your Mom always like this?" For some reason, Linda lied and said, "No". She'd already learned to hide pretty well. She followed an unspoken rule: you don't talk about what goes on inside your house. This occasion was Linda's first official "runaway". They didn't do anything to her this time though.

After that incident, Linda had a brilliant idea. There was a concrete structure, a culvert in the wash. She started saving her money and buying food to store there. She thought when she stored enough food she may be able to stay there sometimes, not forever of course, but sometimes. Her hopes were dashed after the next big rainstorm washed all her food away.

Linda didn't live in this house very long. Pretty soon the family moved again, around the corner to Judd Street.

So these are my random memories of childhood, living life as little Linda.

7

Welcome to the teenage years. Now life starts getting interesting. Fasten your seat belts because this is the E-Ticket (a ticket for a wild ride at Disneyland for any readers who are too young to know). Join me for the journey if you like.

For one thing, Larry left home. He quit high school and joined the Air Force. We shared one wonderful evening before he left. Larry, his girlfriend, Judy, his friend, John and I drove down to Hollywood Blvd for the Fourth of July. Judy attended beauty school and did her hair red, white and blue for the occasion. She did my hair royal blue and put it up in a beehive. I got silly that night and pretended to pry a penny out of a footprint on the Hollywood Walk of Fame with a can opener. Lucky for me, I didn't get arrested for attempting to deface public property. I had fun that night. It was so nice of Larry to take me. Mom yelled at me when we got home late but it was worth it.

Judy became part of our family and remained so even after she and Larry broke up. I had my first drinking experience with her. She took me to the beach with her girlfriends and they brought wine, which she let me drink. Unfortunately, I got a little tipsy and ran into the ocean with a wine bottle in my hand. A wave knocked me over, but I came up laughing, holding the bottle up in the air, saying, "Don't worry, I've still got it!" Except I didn't. In my hand was the neck, the rest of the bottle was somewhere in the ocean. I decided I didn't like drinking.

Next, Mom left home. No one gave any explanation, she was just gone and Stevie and I stayed with Dad. Dad was gone a lot, working and whatever, so it was my turn to watch Stevie. He was a pretty good kid. I didn't have any problems with him that I can recall. Well, except that one time I threw a pair of pliers at him. I can't remember why. Thankfully, I missed him but the pliers did hit the television.

Truthfully, I didn't miss my mom. Things around the house were much quieter and more peaceful. Later I learned Mom had met a boyfriend at work and moved out into her own apartment. I don't remember exactly how long Mom was gone, six or nine months, but then everything seems to last six or nine months to me. I don't recall Mom coming to visit me at all during that time though.

I started my first menstrual period shortly after Mom left. So I had to tell my Dad. He was pretty cool about it. He went to the store to buy me the supplies I needed and came home with the Game of Life, a board game. I had bad cramps for a couple of days so I stayed around the house, playing the game with my new best friend, Carol.

A couple of boys starting coming around my house too, like male dogs smelling a female in heat, I guess. Anyway, I liked to dance with them out in the street in front of the house at night. I wasn't interested in doing anything more with boys at that time. Dad was usually not home so I never let boys in the house.

Mom eventually decided to come back home. I rode with her to her apartment to get some of her things. She was so drunk she crashed into a parked car. I saw it coming, almost like we were in slow motion. Mom had an open bottle of whiskey in the car, which she promptly told me to take and hide somewhere. It was a miracle they didn't arrest her. I guess Mom was thrilled about coming back home to us all.

Mom's drinking got worse than ever. It was a very unusual day to come home from school and find her sober. I can still remember that "hung-over, morning-after" smell in her bedroom after a night of drinking and smoking.

Speaking of smoking, my friend Carol and I decided to try it out. She would steal cigarettes from her mother and share them with me. On one occasion, when we didn't have any cigarettes, we rolled up some oregano in notebook paper and smoked that. No Bueno! Somehow Mom found out and yelled at me. It worked. I quit, for a while.

8.

At fifteen years of age, I met my first real boyfriend. One day, Carol and I walked a few miles down to the strip mall in Panorama City. There was a record store there where I could buy my latest favorite 45 rpm record for $1.00. There was also a little café where we liked to have a cherry coke and some fries. I saw a cute guy working there, but I didn't talk to him or anything. However later when we were walking home, this guy pulled up alongside me in his car. He had followed me. They didn't have stalker laws in those days I guess.

His name was Gary. He was seventeen. He kind of looked like Elvis Presley with light brown hair. He had a habit of lifting one eyebrow, just like Elvis. We starting going out, which, amazingly, my parents let me do. We dated for about six months. Everything was very innocent, some kissing, making out even, but nothing more. I was in love! We did silly things like write love notes all over the seats of his car. We saw Elvis movies and listened to music. I finally found someone who cared about me! We were going to get married someday. Favorite song: "**Hey Paula**" by Paul and Paula and "**My Special Angel**" by Bobby Helms.

Everything was good. Then Mom started worrying about what I might be doing with Gary, even though I told her I hadn't done anything wrong. She started cutting back on the freedom she had already given me. She only allowed me to see Gary twice a week. That didn't work for me so I found a solution. I started cutting school and forging my absence notes so I could spend more time with him.

I dropped a forged absence note on my bedroom floor one day. When I got home I found Mom waiting for me at the front door. "Get your a** in here, Linda!" she yelled. She told me to get into my room, followed me in and pushed me down on my bed. Then she took off my shoe and beat me with it.

Gary had driven me home and waited at the front door. She went after him next. In those days our milk was delivered in glass bottles and we left the empties on the front porch for pickup. Mom grabbed one of those empty bottles and chased Gary down the street with it. Somehow he talked her into giving him a chance to say goodbye to me. She called me out of my room to the front door. He asked, "Could we have a moment?" I couldn't believe it! She turned around and walked into the kitchen, leaving us alone! The minute she left our sight, Gary grabbed my arm and said. "Come on, we're getting out of here". And out the front door we went.

This began a four-day journey that ended up in San Francisco. We stopped that night by the beach somewhere along the coast. We were resting and talking about what we were going to do next when suddenly lights were shining behind us. The police arrived and I thought, "*Well, this is it.*" A policeman came around to my side of the car and asked me what I was doing out there so late. I wasn't a very creative liar so I pretended to have laryngitis. Then he talked to Gary and asked him why I lied. Gary told him, "I don't know, she's probably afraid". I'm not sure what else Gary said but they let us go! Unbelievable!

I left the house with nothing and Gary had very little money. So he sold all kinds of things to buy gas and some food for us to eat. He sold things from his car, such as the floor mats and hubcaps. He sold his wallet and his jacket. With nothing left to sell, we drove around to the back of gas stations and took tires that were left back there. Gary managed to find a place that would buy them from us.

Four days later we drove into San Francisco. I will never forget, the song "**South Street**", by the Orlons, playing on the radio as I stared at all the tall buildings in the city. Well, we're here, now what?

Gary decided he needed to call home and let his mother know he was okay. His sister was pregnant and didn't have a husband. His father was dead (except, I found out later, he really wasn't). Gary was the only one working, he explained. So he called. I guess he told her where we were because the police showed up about ten minutes later. Gary couldn't talk his way out of it this time. They took me to Juvenile Hall.

My welcome at Juvenile Hall began with a body search. Then they threw me in the shower. My period was approaching and I had some spotting in my underwear. The attendant made some lovely comments about us "dirty girls from out of town". Next, they took me to a room to be examined by a doctor, which meant: climb up on the cold table and spread your legs. They said they had the right to do that since I was from "out of town". They may have been looking for evidence to charge Gary, I don't know. In any event, it kind of worked in my favor because the doctor discovered I was still a "good girl", as she put it. They were nicer to me after that.

I will never forget the sound of the steel gate of the cell slamming shut, locking me inside. I spent the night in the cell with a girl named Linda Love. She was very friendly, almost too friendly, and talked late into the night. I thought she acted weird and wished she would shut up and leave me alone.

The next day a social worker drove me to the airport as my Dad sent money for them to fly me home. That lady treated me kindly. She even gave me a couple of cigarettes (I was a smoker for real by this time). I trembled as I boarded the plane, probably because of my recurring nightmares about airplanes crashing. I suffered from those, as well as dreams about tidal waves, since early childhood. The tidal waves were the worst. I dreamt of waves about 100 feet high, trying to outrun them, with no escape. Stress maybe? Feeling overwhelmed? Anyway, what a shame I made my first flight alone and under those circumstances.

Mom and Dad picked me up from the airport. Time to face the music. Mom said.

"I understand you smoke now?" She started buying me cartons of cigarettes from then on. She didn't say much more than that. When we got home, I walked straight to my room and pretty much stayed there. I couldn't see Gary, of course. But surprisingly, he came over about a week later and talked to my parents. Somehow, he managed to get them to agree to a visitation schedule of sorts. They allowed him to come over two days a week but I could not leave the house with him.

I refused to go back to school because Carol told me there was a rumor circulating about me. They said I was pregnant. The general opinion was, "with that guy, no wonder." Apparently my boyfriend had a reputation at San Fernando High School. I couldn't face it. And I never really felt safe there anyway. You needed to be careful going into the girl's bathroom if you happened to be white. A very large Hispanic girl assaulted me once in the girl's locker room. She claimed I had thrown my towel at her, I hadn't but it was a good excuse to grab my shirt and threaten me, accusing me of calling her a B****. Another time, a girl three times my size challenged me to meet her after school in the alley. All my friends told me not to go. "It won't be a fair fight," they said. I believed I had to go. I would never be left alone if I didn't show up. I pulled it off by continually kicking at her so she couldn't get close enough to get a punch in. Eventually, she gave up and left. Ah, the joys of high school. Anyway, I refused to go back to that school!

The problem was the school district wouldn't give me a transfer to another school. They started sending a social worker to our house. Mom, who still drank heavily, became upset with this lady "bugging her." After a month of the lady's visits, Mom started threatening me, "If you don't go back to school you can't see Gary anymore!" I didn't understand the connection but had no doubt she would follow through. I couldn't lose him! He was the only person I loved and trusted. We were going to get married someday.

When Gary came over that night I told him all about it. He said, "Don't worry. I've got it all worked out. I figured out a place to take you where they will never find you. After your parents go to bed, I want you to sneak out and meet me over on Fillmore Street." Foolish girl! Did I ask any questions? Did I even consider what would happen? No, I ran away again. I left with a toothbrush and a pair of pajamas.

So where did he take me? He took me to his house, or rather under his house, to a crawl space, which had a trap door in his bedroom closet. That's where he put me.

Welcome to freedom. For the first four or five days, he would bring me up at night. I needed to be quiet in the daytime because he lived with his mother and sister and he didn't want them to find me. Gary decided it was time he got some more action. I didn't want to but thought I better since I stayed there in his house, I guess. I didn't like it. It was different than when we just kissed. He made me do things I hated. I felt dirty. I lost something I could never regain, not only my virginity, my innocence, but also my ability to trust. Something inside me died. I would never be the same and I would spend the rest of my life trying to come back from that hell.

I don't know if it was due to my reaction to sex or if I smelled bad after five days under the house but he didn't bother me sexually anymore. He had other fun things to do, sick mind games.

Gary kept a big knife under his pillow. He said he kept it there because he would not let anyone take me from him again. One night, after he stopped wanting sex, he pretended to stab himself with the knife. He fell back on the bed pretending he was dead. Frantic, I ran my hand all over his stomach, searching for blood. Finally, I took the knife over to the window and cracked the blind a bit to let in a little light (I wasn't allowed to open the blinds in case someone saw me). The blade was clean! Immediately, Gary lifted his head and calmly asked me, "Are you alright?" How weird. Did he think I stabbed myself? It seemed like he hoped I had.

Another night Gary pretended to be in terrible pain. He held his stomach and moaned. "I just need to hold you." At first, I let him but he squeezed me so tight I thought he would break my ribs. So I made him stop.

Gary decided to 'wrestle' with me one night. He ended up sitting on my stomach on the floor and suddenly reached down and ripped my pants wide open. I wore my pajamas all the time after that.

He spent one night confessing to me about all the girls he'd been with. He acted strange, talking to me as if I was someone else. When he got to me, he referred to me as Linda, like I was not even there. He said, "I never meant to do that to her."

Gary started dating his old girlfriend again. He put a picture of them together on his dresser. One afternoon, I lay under the house watching him through the screen opening in the crawlspace. He was putting seat covers on his car seats. (Remember, we wrote all kinds of love notes all over them.) He had painted my name on the side of his car too, but there was nothing he could do about that now. I guess he had a date. Maybe he hoped I would leave. I could have. It would have been easy to call out to his mother. But then what, go back home? Or would I go to Juvenile Hall this time, as my parents had threatened?

He left the trap door open for me that night. He told me to get out and go take a shower because no one would be home. Instead, I went to the bathroom and found a big bottle of aspirin. Then I walked into the kitchen and got a bottle of coke from the fridge. I took my aspirin and coke back down below, back into the crawl space. I don't know how many aspirins I took, but it was enough that I started hallucinating. I heard a fight at a boxing ring and a voice yelling, "Hit him hard, huh? Hit him hard, huh?" Then I slept. I woke when Gary opened the trap door and found the bottle of aspirin. "How many of these did you take?" he asked. I told him I didn't know. He gave me some takeout food, a change from my daily peanut butter and jelly sandwich, and shut the trap door. The food made me sick, which was a good thing. I vomited everything up, including the pills I had taken. Then I slept some more. When I woke up, I found a stray cat nearby eating my vomit. I wondered if it was the same cat that brought a dead fish down there to eat a couple of days before. I hate cats!

Gary stopped bringing me up at night. He also stopped feeding me at all. Maybe it would be easier for him if I just died. All he would have to do is figure out what to do with the body. I didn't care. I didn't want to go home anyway, back to the house of chaos. If I died down there, it would be okay. Song of my heart: "**Puff, The Magic Dragon**" by Peter, Paul and Mary. Like Puff, I had been abandoned.

I stayed there for two weeks. Then, as it happened, Gary's mother found a pan of water under his bed, which I used to wash. I heard her yelling at him, "Have you been bringing that girl here?" That night he brought me up around midnight. He told me, "You have to go. And you can't tell anyone you were here or my mom will get in trouble. That wouldn't be fair." I was very weak since I hadn't eaten at all in four or five days. I also had a full bladder because I didn't have the strength to crawl to the other side of the crawl space to take care of business. So when I tried to stand up, I fainted. I woke up to Gary shaking me, saying, "Shut up! You've made too much noise already!" Unfortunately, when I passed out, I lost control of my bladder. I soaked my pajamas and his floor. Then he shoved me out his bedroom window. It was my sixteenth birthday.

9.

My brother, Larry lived close by so I decided to walk there. I found a dark spot on the street, checked to make sure no one was around and then changed into my ripped pants. I hid my urine-soaked pajamas in a bush. Don't ask me why. I made it as far as Larry's apartment and collapsed at his front door.

When I got home, the police were waiting. I did as I had been instructed. I lied. I told the police I had walked for two weeks and since I knew what they would do next, I told them I was attacked along the way. The police took me to a hospital where I got the cold table, feet in the stirrups treatment. This time I encountered a creepy doctor who started touching me in a very undoctorly way, asking me if it felt good. I said nothing. I just glared at him. I guess the consensus was something happened to me but it didn't look like rape. That made sense. I hadn't put up a fight. It hurt enough as it was.

Mom had another problem with my story. My shoes were not worn out. She asked, "If you were walking all that time, wouldn't your shoes be worn?" So I came clean. I told the truth, but I made sure to tell them Gary's mother didn't have anything to do with it.

This time I barely escaped Juvenile Hall. They almost made me a ward of the court. Wouldn't it have been ironic if they had sent me to that place with the gray walls in Sylmar? I received six months probation for juvenile delinquency. I saw Gary in the hallway at court that day. I don't know what kind of punishment he received, if any. I reported to a probation officer once a month. I attended continuation school in Van Nuys since I still refused to go back to San Fernando High. They finally gave me a transfer to Van Nuys High the following semester.

The local paper ran an article talking about my "bizarre account". The article described how I talked this poor boy into letting me stay under his house and how I amused myself by playing with the cats while down there. I guess that is what Gary told them. The reporter never asked me what happened.

I wasn't allowed out of the house for a long time, except to go to school, which suited me just fine. I didn't want to go out anyway. I stayed in the family room, which was very dark since Mom always kept all the blinds shut. That was fine with me too. I spent many hours in the family room or in my bedroom. I tried hitting the pills a couple times but never succeeded. I couldn't keep enough of them in my stomach. They wouldn't stay down. I also tried poking at some veins a couple times but wasn't courageous enough to do the job right. I scratched my knuckles raw at one point. No one seemed to notice any of it. It was a dark, dark time.

Teenagers have a tendency to believe that the way they feel at that moment will never change. They will always feel that way. Perhaps that is the reason there is so much teenage suicide. I should have received some counseling.

A boy named Frank, who I knew from junior high school, started coming around. He must have read the article in the newspaper. They didn't use my name, of course, since I was a minor, but somehow he knew. He tried to kiss me one day. Mom saw it and yelled, "I saw that, you whore!" which pretty much told me what she thought of me. She glared at me, as only she knew how to do. (My kids think my "eyebrow look" is bad) Anyway, Frank tried to do more than kiss me one day but I didn't let him. He complained, "Well you did it with him, why won't you do it with me?" I should have known. I went steady with him for a short time in junior high but one day, walking home through the wash, he got mad at me because I wouldn't kiss him. I didn't want to make out in the wash. He got so mad he tore his ring off the chain hanging around my neck (the token of going steady in those days). It's always about sex, isn't it? This time I sent him packing.

That summer I got a job at Grant's Department Store in the soda fountain. I came back to life somewhat. Then as I rode the bus to work one day, sitting in the front seat that faced the side of the bus, the door opened and there was Gary. He was sitting in his car directly across from me at a gas station, looking right back at me. He must have followed the bus because the next day he came into the soda fountain, with a girl on his arm. I asked the lady I worked with to go take care of them so I wouldn't have to. I don't know why he would do that. Did he deliberately try to hurt me? How cruel could someone be? Anyway, I didn't give him the satisfaction of having to serve him. And that was the last time I ever saw him.

I saved all my earnings that summer and bought my first car, a little blue Ford.

Mom allowed me to drive it once but unfortunately, I scratched a car trying to back out of a parking space. Mom took my car and kept it for herself. She never mentioned it. I never dared to ask for a second chance. I never asked for my car back. I didn't drive again until after I moved out of the house.

I made a decision that I would never run away again. I would have to stick it out until I turned eighteen years old. Then I would leave, legally. I also made a decision to start applying myself to schoolwork. My grades were always okay before all this happened but nothing stellar. For the next year and a half, I made straight 'A's'. I discovered I really liked bookkeeping. Could be I harbored a secret need to balance my accounts. I also loved choir. No surprise there. Most importantly, I decided I would survive. I would live and not die!

(NOTE: I have since forgiven Gary. He was a seventeen-year-old kid with raging hormones. He obviously had issues. While under his house, I heard his father, who was supposed to be dead, show up drunk and causing a scene. I pray Gary found peace in his life.)

10.

Later that fall, life took an unexpected turn. We were supposed to go to Disneyland when Dad got home from work but he got home too late. Mom and Dad decided to take us to Corriganville Movie Ranch instead. Corriganville was a small western town up in the area then known as Santa Susana (it is now considered the east end of Simi Valley). They used to shoot movies there. They also performed live shows for the public on the weekends, such as the Gunfight at the OK Corral, The Shooting of Belle Starr and the Killing of Billy the Kid. I saw Stevie go up to Crash Corrigan and ask him for his autograph so I thought I would do the same. I simply couldn't believe it when Mr. Corrigan asked me if I would like to work there! I didn't know if it meant I would be a star or what but I didn't care. It would be exciting! Mr. Corrigan spoke with my parents and explained the details and so I was hired. My salary was five dollars a weekend. Bring your own costumes.

We used to take the Santa Susana Pass up to "the ranch" as we called it. The 118 Freeway didn't go through until years later. This area had a most unusual landscape with huge boulders everywhere. One large boulder that appeared to be propped up on top of a hill had the words "Lost World" painted on it. I saw it every weekend as we drove there and that is exactly how I viewed the ranch. A lost world! I could escape my dreary world and go to another, one of make-believe. I got to dress up in costumes and be somebody else for a while. Corriganville was a healing place for me. My Mom took me shopping in thrift stores for clothing that I used as costumes. She even made me a beautiful blue western dress with her own hands. I really appreciated that. It made me feel loved.

I started out working as a background actor but before long they let me start doing some stunt work. I did a running fall in a show about a bank robbery. One time during that show I landed on a burning cigarette butt. Fortunately for me, one of the cowboys noticed and pretended to kick my dead body in order to move me off of the cigarette.

I also tumbled down a hill in the Shooting of Belle Starr and learned the hard way to be careful not to land on the railroad tracks at the bottom of the hill. It's hard to stay dead with burning, red-hot metal under you!

My favorite show was The Shooting Of Billy the Kid. I dressed up as an Indian girl named Delafina, Billy the Kid's girlfriend. It was my favorite role. I hid behind dark make-up and a black wig. I screamed and yelled after Billy was shot, expressed real emotion, as I could never do in real life.

One stunt they wouldn't let me do was a roof fall… because I was a girl. But I wanted to do a roof fall. One night, my opportunity came. A lot of the families of the actors would party all day in the Silver Dollar Saloon and sometimes into the night, including my family. On one of those nights, as everyone drank beer and had a good time, I had an idea. I decided to play a game of "Follow the Leader", the leader being me. It was great fun! I had a long line of people behind me, climbing over the tables, the bar, and out the swinging doors, down the street to the back of the General Store. I climbed up the ladder with my stunt instructor, Cherokee Jim, right behind me. I almost changed my mind when I got to the edge of the roof and looked down at the ground below, but Cherokee said, "Oh no, you're up here now, you're going! Take the fall with the full length of the side of your body and tuck your arms out of the way." And so I did. So did my Dad, who was following right behind me. Such fun! Thankfully, neither one of us got hurt.

There were two guys working at the ranch who caught my attention. The first one was Tommy. He kind of reminded me of Paul McCartney. He played guitar, sang, and did impressions. The girls were crazy about him. As I walked down the street, shortly after my arrival, Tommy allegedly pointed me out to the other person of interest, Rick Richards. Rick's response was, "Tommy, she's just a *********** Bubblegummer".

I thought Tommy was cute and very talented but clearly a player. I certainly didn't need one of those in my life. I didn't want any romantic interest. I wasn't ready. This guy Rick though, it seemed he was always around, rescuing me from some situation or another. Like the day I started my period and was unprepared. The stupid tampon machine wouldn't work! Rick appeared out of nowhere. He asked me what was wrong, and strangely, instead of cutting him off with my usual, "Nothing", I told him. He packed me up in his car and took me to the store to get what I needed.

Then there was the day when I had a fight with my mom. I was faring better these days, especially at the ranch, but I still struggled with deep depression. Rick took me behind the sheriff's office and sat down on a table with me to talk. That day, for some reason, I told him everything that happened to me, about my home life and everything I felt about it all. I poured out my heart to him. He seemed so understanding, maybe because he experienced a rough childhood as well. He was five years older than me and seemed like a big brother, looking out for me, protecting me. And so we began hanging out together at the ranch.

Eventually, Rick asked me to go to a movie with him. He seemed completely shocked when I told him he would have to ask my parents! After all, I was only sixteen and came with some history. Rick would later claim our relationship was strictly platonic, not romantic at all. But he sure seemed interested in spending time with me. And he did indeed ask my parents' permission to take me out. Maybe he thought he could fix this broken little Bubblegummer.

11.

For the next year and a half, I attended Simi Valley High School and studied hard. I loved their choir and participated in various competitions. My dad bought me a guitar and some guitar lessons. When I wasn't studying I practiced guitar in my room. Or I read books, or Archie comic books, my other love. I ate sunflower seeds until my tongue was bumpy from the salt. On the weekends I worked at the ranch during the day and dated Rick at night.

The summer of 1964, the ranch opened to the public during the week. So I worked there every day. Rick worked a regular job during the week at Aerospace. He had been in the military, 82nd Airborne, and had a security clearance. Anyway, with Rick not around during the week, Tommy made his presence known. He wanted to hang out. I discovered Rick was spending time with some lady at his acting school during the week. That kind of hurt since we were spending a lot of time together, so I figured I would hang out with Tommy. Why not?

We had some fun times. Tommy drove a black hearse in which he carried all his musical equipment. One day I had a brilliant idea. What if Tommy climbed into his hearse and discovered a body in the back? So I took some old costumes and stuffed them with straw. The back of Tommy's hearse wasn't locked so I had no problem sneaking the body in there. I couldn't wait until Tommy got in his car and found it. I'm not sure he thought it all that funny but I sure did.

There was an old deserted Opera House at the ranch with a piano in it. I took my guitar music there in between shows and tried to teach myself to play. That was the instrument I really wanted to play but my parents couldn't afford a piano. I actually made some progress on my own and had beautiful alone time in the process.

Another cool thing happened that summer. They filmed a "B" western called "Deadwood 76" at the ranch. They cast me as a dance hall girl working mostly background. I found the video online years later and purchased it. I was surprised to see I actually got a lot of screen time. I had a scene in which the girls in the saloon became upset with someone over something. I think I played an angry girl pretty well. The director of the film later called me to interview for their next film, which would be filmed in Las Vegas. It was not going to be a western but rather something about a wayward girl getting in trouble. Hmm, typecasting? Anyway, they wanted me for the lead but it involved some nudity. Dad accompanied me to the interview and he seemed to be okay with the nude scene. At least, he didn't say anything about it. But the idea didn't work for me. I knew I couldn't get naked in front of a bunch of people on the set and I couldn't imagine having people seeing me on the screen that way.

Back at the ranch, the time came to have a discussion with Rick and tell him I was hanging out with Tommy. I didn't think he would care since he had his girlfriend at his acting school, but much to my surprise, he said, "Okay, how about if we go steady?" What? He gave me his 82nd Airborne wings as a token. It seemed like the right decision. It wasn't like Tommy and I were serious or anything. But then I needed to let Tommy know. He smiled and wished us luck.

Going steady eventually became an engagement. I don't remember exactly how or the exact moment it happened. It just sort of evolved. In the meantime, the ranch seemed to be changing. A lot of bikers were coming out there every weekend, and things were getting a little rough. So, Rick decided we should stop working there. "It served its purpose," he said.

Rick seemed to handle my mom pretty well, for the most part. He didn't seem horrified by her drinking. He called her "Stella", using his Marlon Brando voice. She seemed to like him pretty well too until she didn't. As our wedding day approached things started getting more difficult. Mom decided I might be doing things with Rick that I shouldn't. She threatened to have Rick charged with statutory rape. I remember one particular night, sitting in the overstuffed chair that Rick called "Pregnant Lucy." I listened to Mom on her rant, screaming and yelling. I sat there trying my best to shut out the sound of her voice. How nice it would be to not hear her voice! Ironically, Mom had no grounds. Rick was always a perfect gentleman with me, which was probably a smart decision on his part.

12.

In June 1965, I graduated from high school with honors and a Bank of America award in Business. Rick and I were married in July at the Wayfarer's Chapel in Palos Verdes, a beautiful, all-glass church designed by Frank Lloyd Wright. I became Linda Richards. I was excited to begin my new life and so very happy to be leaving home! Rick would later say he almost changed his mind. He almost turned around on the way to the church because he was so scared. We held our reception at the Skytrails Restaurant at the Van Nuys Airport where my mom used to work. I understand the reception became an unruly affair, which thankfully I missed. Rick and I left early to begin our trip to Mammoth Lakes for our honeymoon. We saw evidence of the merriment when we returned to our new apartment. One of Dad's friends helped bring the wedding gifts to our place afterward and thought it would be funny to remove and hide all the light bulbs in the place. We found them in the toilet tank.

We enjoyed our honeymoon until we both came down with the flu and needed to leave early. The elevation in Mammoth didn't help our illness. I wasn't too freaked out by the additional activities in our relationship although it did seem like Rick was interested in a lot more frequency than I expected. *"I will warm up to this. I just need time. It's not that I don't like it. I just need to learn trust, I think."* Many years later though, I read a book Rick wrote in which he said he knew he made a mistake the first week we were married. I don't know what he expected.

We returned to our new, one-bedroom apartment in Panorama City, a quiet little place. Rick bought me a little Corvair to drive. Life was good. I felt hopeful. I started attending a modeling school and even started doing some modeling work. I didn't love modeling though. I found it to be mindless work, stand around and look pretty and all. And it is possible that I got a bad taste in my mouth for modeling when I went on a modeling tour with an old geezer that required me to wear beaded evening gowns for the buyers in department stores. We drove to Arizona, Texas and Oklahoma. Texas scared me to death with its lightning storms and not a mountain in sight. The killer, though, was at a Neiman Marcus store in Oklahoma City. The old geezer didn't like my hair. It wasn't sophisticated enough so I had to wear a wig. The wig didn't fit me quite right so on top of my head I had pinned a wad of toilet paper. I had to run quickly back and forth from the changing room to the buyer's room. On my last trip to the changing room, someone had moved a clothing rack in my path and left it there. Instead of running around it, I tried to duck and run under it. Somehow my wig got caught on a hook on the rack and I was left standing in front of a laughing crowd with my toilet paper wad on my head. No, I don't think I like modeling.

Then I found out Lee Grant was teaching acting classes. I grew up watching her on Peyton Place and loved her! She was always my favorite character on the show. I joined her class with much excitement. I later got an agent and took the professional name 'Lynn James'. I would be known as 'Lynn' for many years, long after I quit acting.

Rick thought it would be a good idea for me to take the classes so I would understand "his dream". But I found freedom studying with Lee… for myself. I discovered I could delve deep and play characters with emotions that I never expressed in real life. I especially loved the sassy characters. My favorite role was the lead in Dinner At Eight, which was definitely not an ingénue role.

13.

Rick managed to lose his job at Aerospace after just a few months of marriage. He got into a fight with his boss and an altercation of some sort ensued. So he decided to sell life insurance. That way he would have a flexible schedule and be free to pursue his dream to become an actor. The only problem was he wasn't any good at selling insurance. He thought those poor people couldn't afford to buy this insurance so he decided he wouldn't try to sell it to them. We lasted six months in that apartment. My Corvair was repossessed as well.

Rick found a perfect solution to our dilemma. His friend, Bob lived in the Hollywood Hills, Laurel Canyon to be exact, otherwise known as "Reefer Hill". Bob had a "guest house" behind his place, which he agreed to rent it to us for only $75 a month. I was in for quite a shock. The guesthouse consisted of one room, a tiny bathroom and a tiny kitchen just big enough for a sink, an apartment size stove, and apartment size fridge. The floor in the living room/bedroom was a concrete slab with a big crack down the center. It didn't exactly have a roof so they would have to build one. Also, there were no steps up the hill to get to this place. They would have to build those too. Ultimately, they had to build them twice because in the first attempt the steps weren't wide enough to walk on.

I could not believe Rick wanted to move me into this place! I can't even describe how it made me feel. Devalued? Worthless? Well yes, but more than that. I felt betrayed, again. What happened to my protector? This was my first clue that Rick's "dream" would always take precedence over everything. That may have been the beginning of a crack in our relationship, which would become as deep as the crack in that concrete slab floor. But in my usual fashion, I retreated inside myself. I did what I was expected to do. We moved to the guesthouse on Weepah Way, on Reefer Hill.

I received quite an education living in this place. As it turned out, Bob was gay and entertained lovers around the house all the time. I had never been exposed to that before. I had never been exposed to drugs before either. I never drank alcohol, mainly because of my experience with my mother. I thought smoking marijuana was something 'beatniks' did.

One night, Rick called me down to the "big house". Rick, Bob, and his current friend were sitting smoking weed. Rick wanted me to try it. I didn't want to do it, but after much coaching, I finally took a couple of hits. Out of nowhere, I started laughing hysterically. I couldn't stop. That scared me so much I started crying hysterically. It freaked me out. I retreated to the guesthouse to lie down on our bed, which was just a rollaway in the couch. That was all the little room could accommodate. I tried to sleep it off.

Rick spent the next few weeks trying to get me to smoke weed again. I told him, "I never want to smoke that stuff again" He kept insisting, "You just have to get used to it." I gave in eventually and got so used to it, I ended up smoking pot every day for about a year and a half. Bob's friend, Monty, became our dealer. All the guys, including Monty, would not give me anything stronger than pot though because I was so sensitive. I smoked and watched the walls breathe. I smoked and watched my poodle turn into a wild boar. I smoked and watched her puppies burn in the fireplace. I smoked and became a robot.

I never visited my mom during this period but Dad came to see me once. I don't remember how it happened but Dad ended up smoking a joint with us. That was certainly a surprise.

I felt bad for little Stevie, leaving him behind, alone with Mom. Years later, he told me things got much worse after I left. He used to go out into the garage and sniff glue. I guess that was his escape.

I began to see the extent of Rick's anger in this place. He never hit me or harmed me physically but he did put several holes in the walls. His violence scared me. Again I found myself keeping my mouth shut and trying to stay out of the way.

Rick performed in a play at the theatre where he studied and invited me to come. He played a clown and the role required him to dance and play. My heart sank as I watched him. He wasn't very good. Actually, I thought he was terrible. *"This man's dream is to be an actor! How is this ever going to work? Well, hopefully, it is just this particular role."* It sure didn't make it any easier to support 'his dream' though.

Rick also smoked pot every day. He would start the moment he woke up in the morning. He also didn't work. We didn't have money for the rent. So it was up to me. I got a job at the telephone company as a switchboard operator. I worked the appropriately named graveyard shift, which did not do great wonders for my health, physically or mentally. Neither did having people scream at me on the phone all night. I eventually took a stress leave. That required my going to counseling for a while which must have been somewhat helpful because I came to a couple of decisions… no more marijuana for me and I needed to get out of this dump.

14.

We moved to a duplex on Westbourne Drive in West Hollywood. I was happy to be out of the guesthouse, a.k.a. the shack, but even so it took me a month to unpack the boxes of kitchen dishes. Rick finally asked me when I thought I might to get around to it. My mind was elsewhere, I guess.

For my twenty-first birthday, Rick took me to a Nina Simone concert at the Whiskey-A-Go-Go in Hollywood. I loved Nina. She played my kind of music, moody, and angry. I was legal now and could drink if I wanted. But I declined, not my thing.

At this point in my life, I needed more. No longer high all the time, I found my soul was pretty empty. So I began the proverbial search 'for more'. I got into astrology, psychics, transcendental meditation, even the Ouija Board, but more about that later. Favorite music: anything Beatles.

I got a call to audition for Peyton Place. I didn't know if that came about because of my agent or my teacher, Lee Grant, but I got excited. I performed my favorite scene from Dinner At Eight, my sassy scene. The producers liked it, but since they were casting an ingénue, they asked me to come back to do a scene from the Glass Menagerie. They wanted me to play the role of the crippled girl. Umm, it was not my favorite, much too vulnerable. I spent a couple of weeks preparing. Rick performed the scene with me. Unfortunately, the night before my audition our old friend Monty came by with some pills he thought we would like. Why did I take it? I have no idea. Foolish girl! As it turned out, it was speed. I didn't sleep all night. So when I did my scene the next day my hands shook for real. I wasn't acting.

They asked me to do a screen test, which I did, but ultimately they gave the part to someone else. Six months later, however, they called me back and, based on my screen test, offered me the part of Lydia. It consisted mostly of background work but it was a semi-running role that kept me working for about a year or so. I'm not sure Rick was too thrilled with the fact that I actually enjoyed a little success. I wonder if he hoped they would hire him instead. Or perhaps he just didn't like being sober, which, for the most part, we were. Our days of "Wine and Roses" were coming to an end (a movie popular in those days about two people whose relationship was based on substance abuse). In any event, things between us were tense.

I started visiting my mom once in a while, not because anything had changed, but because she was my mother. Mom brought out an Ouija Board one day. We sat and played with it and supposedly contacted my grandfather. He told me to "Love God". I thought the whole thing was pretty cool so I asked to borrow it. I took it home and played it with Rick. We contacted 'my grandfather'. We asked him about our marriage. The answer was we were going to break up. Rick asked when and the answer was Thursday. The following Thursday, Rick packed his things and left. We never even discussed it. Weird! I guess neither one of us was very happy.

15.

I was excited to begin my single life. I was on my own for the first time. It didn't last long though. One night, I went with a friend from acting class to The Factory, a private club located about a mile from my place. My friend told me her mother dated Peter Lawford. That's why we were able to get in the club. It was quite a night. I sat at a table of celebrities. Joey Bishop sat across from me but was quite rude. I didn't care much for him. Jim Brown, the football player asked me to dance. Afterward, I drove with my friend back to her house in Westwood to get my car and then drove home. Approaching a signal back near The Factory, I saw a flashing yellow light and a car coming into the intersection. My last memory is going for my brake. I woke up lying in the street. A girl, coming from the opposite direction, ran the flashing red light.

I woke up looking into the face of Dickie Smothers. "Are you alright?" he asked. "I saw it happen." He sat me down in his Rolls Royce and told me to stay there. He left to call an ambulance (we didn't have cell phones in those days). I must have been in shock because I immediately got out of his car and started wandering around my little

Volkswagen, repeating, "Oh, my head! Oh, my car." I saw the left front end smashed in, also the left rear end. The window on the driver's side was smashed out. I found one of my shoes in the back seat and there was a shoe mark on the ceiling. I had no memory of the accident, except for a vague recollection of moving my foot out of the way of a wheel. My pretty pink and purple dress had a large black scuffmark on the butt.

I called Rick from the hospital and he came to take me home. I could not move my body at all the next day. So guess where I went? Mom's house! I lay in bed for two weeks, except for a visit to the doctor. My entire body suffered severe whiplash. I had to wear a neck collar and back brace for six months, which covered me from my neck down to the bottom of my hips. The doctor seemed surprised he did not have to perform surgery. He said he expected the disc in my lower back to herniate. He also said I would likely have problems with arthritis later in life.

16.

When I recovered sufficiently to be alone again, I decided to change my living situation. I didn't want to go back to the duplex. I wanted to make a fresh start. I found a cute little place in the Hollywood Hills above the Cahuenga Pass. It was a downstairs apartment in an elderly man's house but with a private entrance. I enjoyed the security of knowing someone lived close by, yet had complete privacy. There were also beautiful flowers everywhere! I loved it!

Rick and I talked sometimes. We were friends. We weren't angry at each other. We never talked about getting a divorce. But I knew he was seeing some girl and he happily talked about his escapades with another actress in his class. I didn't date for quite a while but finally I did go to see a band with a friend of mine from acting class. The name of the band was "Hearts and Flowers". I thought the lead singer, Larry, was the cutest! And so talented! So I returned to the club with another friend. Then I decided to go back by myself. By this time he recognized me (not hard to do with my neck collar on) and we ended up talking. We got together a few times. He performed at the Ice House in Pasadena and invited me to come. He also invited me to a recording session that he produced. We ate lunch one day and discussed our experiences with the Ouija Board. He told me he lost a close friend and contacted him on the board. His friend told him, "Love God." I almost lost it right there in the restaurant. Larry gave me copies of his two albums. He autographed one: "Dear Lynn, of the Pisces fame, remember not the sorrow but sometimes the name."

I liked Larry but things came to an end when he came over to my apartment. He started making the moves much too fast for me. The end.

I kept my relationship with the Ouija Board for a while though. I even played with it all by myself and I knew that thing, the planchette, moved because I sure wasn't doing it. All I did was place my fingers on it and it took off. It was fun at first, until one day, the thing started moving erratically all over the board, out of control. It acted like some kind of angry, crazy spirit. It scared me. I had no idea what kind of power I was dealing with so I threw it in the trash.

II

IN THE COCOON

The cocoon, properly called the chrysalis, is the hard-shell covering of the pupa. The butterfly lives in this cocoon while it is in its preparatory, transitional state.

17.

Rick called me one day and told me he met a guy on the street who invited him to a Buddhist meeting. He wanted to know if I wanted to go with him and check it out. I still practiced Transcendental Meditation but I was open and still searching. I liked meditation although I spent a lot of time wondering if I would experience some kind of astral projection. I vacillated back and forth between hoping I would and fearing it actually would happen. It was distracting.

When we arrived at the meeting, which was held at someone's house, we first noticed all the shoes outside the front door. Rick immediately had a problem with that. "I'm not taking off my shoes!" He changed his mind when we entered the room and saw everyone sitting on the floor. We sat and listened to people chant strange words to a scroll hanging in a box. Weird! Then they shared their experiences with Buddhism and how it changed their lives. The speaker talked about "testing" this chanting like a scientist. You didn't have to give up anything you believed in, just add this to your life and try it. He told us, "If you chant these words, you will get anything you want, physically, spiritually or materially." We both decided to try it but we weren't joining anything!

I started chanting the words, here and there, and something started to happen immediately. When I would lay down at night to go to sleep and get to that in-between place of not asleep but not awake, I would see these creatures yelling at me, taunting me. Sometimes they were spinning on an electrical wire, singing and mocking me. It made me crazy. One of the Buddhist girls, who had been assigned to look after me, took me to see a Senior Leader. This guy explained, "This is probably happening because you are meditating and you are cutting your karma by chanting because you are reducing the eventual negative effect of your heretical practice of meditation." His advice was to stop meditating immediately and chant for this thing to go away. I really wanted to sleep so I followed his 'guidance'. The visitations, or whatever they were, stopped immediately. This was my first "actual proof", as the Buddhists called it. Now one has to wonder, did the meditation cause the problem or the chanting since it never happened before? The leader also encouraged me to take the next step and get my own scroll.

As I continued to chant, I had another very strange experience. I heard this voice in my head, "You should not put idols before the Lord, your God." It was more of a thought than a voice, but not my thought. It certainly wasn't something I would ever think. It is scripture, as it turns out, but I didn't know that at the time. I heard this 'voice' several times and it found it unsettling. However, my new Buddhists friends assured me this scroll was not an idol but represented my very own enlightened condition of life, the true object of worship. I didn't know God at the time. I had no understanding of Him, no relationship. So I ignored His voice. I got my scroll and started chanting to it, offering incense, candles, and fruit to my enlightened self, in the box on the wall, which was not an idol. And so, in June 1968, I began what would become a twenty-year journey with Buddhism and the organization. Having given me a free choice, God let me go, for a time.

Shortly after, I encountered a problem with my lovely little apartment. It flooded. Guess where I had to go? Back to Mom's house. Mom and Dad recently moved back to the San Fernando Valley. Their current house had something like a greenhouse behind the garage. That's where I stayed. At least I had a little distance. Mom seemed happy to have me there, at first. She even let me put my scroll up in there even though she didn't agree with this new chanting business. But it didn't take long for her to become unhappy

33

with my going out to Buddhist meetings every night and sleeping later in the morning than she thought I should. And she let me know.

18

The Buddhists were having a convention in Hawaii in August of that year. They encouraged Rick and me to chant for the money to go. "This will be a great test of the power of chanting," they said. A few weeks later we received a tax refund, so we decided to go. Who doesn't want to go to Hawaii? "Another actual proof", they said. Never mind the fact that we already had a tax refund coming.

As I disembarked from the airplane in Hawaii, I encountered the most stifling humidity I had ever experienced! Our journey began as buses took us to a warehouse on Pier something or other, definitely not a hotel. This pier was located about five miles or so away from the lovely beaches. There was not a beach in sight. The warehouse was a two-story building, one floor for the men and one for the women, with army cots to sleep on. The women's bathroom leaked down onto the men's floor. Uh, this is not what I signed up for! Another thing, everyone had to wear uniforms, aloha shirts for the guys and muumuus for the women. Uniforms! What's up with that?

We were not pleased with the food they served at the warehouse. Rick and I were vegetarians. Their deli sandwiches were not thrilling. Rick became quite upset and asked to speak to the man in charge. They took him to Mr. K. When Rick explained his displeasure, Mr. K told him, "Hey Buddy, why don't you go up in the mountains and find a banana!" So we got a cab and took off.

During our time in Hawaii, Rick and I spent a lot of time together, mainly because we didn't want to be around the people of the organization. We got along surprisingly well, which one day lead to a conversation about whether they had such a thing as a Buddhist wedding. Rick started talking about how he felt love for the first time, which he attributed to the chanting. When we arrived back at the warehouse that day, someone started talking to us about Buddhists weddings. Ok, weird!

Another day, we were at the beach and thought we heard chanting, but we were far away from the pier. When we got back, someone asked us. "Have you ever thought you heard chanting when you knew you weren't anywhere near a place where people were chanting? Did you know what you are hearing is the rhythm of the universe?" Very mystical!

On our last day in Hawaii, we attended a large meeting in the warehouse, with everyone chanting together. All of a sudden, someone came running up to the leader, yelling, "There's a double rainbow from one end of the pier to the other!" Another sign! I later discovered double rainbows are not an unusual experience in Hawaii at all, but at the time we considered it yet another 'actual proof'.

All of these experiences were very exciting, so Rick and I continued to chant. We also got back together and marked the occasion with a Buddhist wedding ceremony. He wore his aloha shirt, and I wore my muumuu.

19.

We rented a little house right above the Cahuenga Pass, my old neighborhood. It was small but quaint. We were making a fresh start. Rick worked at some job or another but after a few months, he quit. Several months later, Rick was still not working. Again I received guidance from a senior leader. He said, "Well if he won't work, you better go get a job. Somebody has to work." Worst advice ever! It set the tone for the next 17 years of marriage.

By this time, I was well aware that guidance from a senior leader was golden. You follow guidance! Otherwise, the universe will punish you! So I got a job as a bookkeeper in a stationary store in Santa Monica, making $300 per month. It paid the rent.

This development meant I was no longer available for any acting interviews or jobs. So I advised my manager I was quitting. Somebody needed to work a real job. My manager was not thrilled. Neither was Lee Grant. My manager informed me, "In that case, you owe me money from your work on Peyton Place". He never took commissions from me when I was working, saying, "We will worry about that when you are rich and famous." Well, now I would not be rich or famous. I refused to pay him, especially since he didn't even get me the job. I got the job because of my screen test. I hadn't signed with him until later. Regardless, he sued me.

By this time my brother, Larry was attending law school. He could not represent me since he wasn't an attorney yet but offered to help me with the paperwork and legal argument. The case involved enough money that it didn't qualify for small claims court, but rather was heard in the municipal court (now considered Superior Court). At trial, I not only testified but also cross-examined my manager, who had shown up in his fancy suit and diamond rings. I made the opening and closing arguments. I loved it! I fought for justice! And I won! I loved it so much I wanted to go to law school right then and there. Unfortunately, I received guidance from Mr. K. He told me it was not good for a marriage for a woman to be more successful than the husband… so forget it. *"I'm kind of already more successful than him since I'm the only one who works. What's the difference?"* I followed guidance and forgot about it, for twenty-six years.

20.

After practicing Buddhism for several months, the senior leaders decided Rick and I should become leaders, honchos, which meant we would be responsible for encouraging several people. After practicing for about ten months, they wanted to promote us to district leaders, responsible for about thirty people. My reaction was not good. I argued, "I am not capable of being in that position. I hardly know anything about Buddhism!" I didn't want that kind of responsibility. But, as usual, my leader knew better (and you must follow your leader's guidance) and so we were appointed and anointed.

Holding that position meant we held meetings at our house. The only problem was people sat on the floor in the meetings. We had a hardwood floor and couldn't afford a carpet. Rick came up with a solution. He drove around to various carpeting stores asking for samples. He proceeded to glue the samples down to carpet padding, at least for about half of the room. The gluing process got a little too tedious so Rick decided to nail the rest of the samples directly on to the hardwood floor and we had a most unusual multi-colored, multi-layered, wall-to-wall carpet. I'll bet the landlord was thrilled to discover his artwork after we moved!

Rick decided he wanted to help me with my "fear" of cats. He brought home a Burmese cat without asking me. This cat was nuts! It would run into the bedroom and crawl up the curtains and dive-bomb into the waterbed. It would also run into the bathroom and dive-bomb into the toilet. Trashcans were another a favorite. I didn't love it. One day the cat made the mistake of jumping up on our Buddhist altar. Maybe it wanted to join the candles, incense, and fruit as an offering to the scroll in the box on the wall, our enlightened selves, which was not an idol. Rick picked it up and threw it against the wall. He broke the cat's hip. He was kind enough to take it to a vet and have it put down. At least he told me that's what he did. Rick was still dealing with some anger issues.

As a district leader I learned we were expected to not only have our "Shakabuku" meetings in our home every night, but we had to attend leader's meetings, usually held afterward. When we didn't have the leader's meetings, we visited with members until late into the night. Thus, began a pattern of sleeping only 4-5 hours every night for many years to come. The organization was quite militant in this regard. This is what you did if you were a leader. Shakabuku, we were told, meant introducing people to the practice of Buddhism. I found out years later that the literal translation is "subdue and break". I was particularly delighted with the requirement of 'Street Shakabuku'. Go out and approach strangers on the street and tell them about Buddhism. Lovely.

Shakabuku was the highest priority to leadership since they believed it to be the path to Kosenrufu or world peace. Their theory was we would have world peace in only twenty years by getting a certain percentage of the population to chant. They didn't need everyone to chant, just this percentage, around 80%.

I also learned it was not true that you can believe anything you want and still be a Buddhist, at least not a leader. For example, you certainly would not believe in God. That would be stupid. "God is just a fairytale... pie in the sky after you die. You become your own god, which is even better!" You don't have to bow down to anyone or anything, except your scroll, of course, and possibly your senior leaders. The president of the lay organization in Japan was the subject of much admiration. People followed him like a movie star. He even required bodyguards. People would lock arms and sings songs to and about him, "Sensei", which means 'Master'. "You create your own destiny through the universal law of cause and effect and change your destiny by making the highest cause, which is chanting," they said. Sounds kind of familiar. Wasn't there something similar said in the Garden of Eden? "You shall be like God." Truly, there is nothing new under the sun.

21.

After working at my bookkeeping job for about nine months, I received a job offer at Fremont Indemnity, a worker's compensation insurance company, as an Audit Reviewer trainee. It meant more money, $375 a month. That was an increase of $75 a month, a huge raise to me at the time. More importantly, it opened a door to a new career. I would go on to make good money and eventually work as an outside auditor, a man's domain in those days. I liked the work too. It was a combination of numbers (I love to balance the books) and insurance law (I love to analyze).

The following year, 1969, the Buddhists held a pilgrimage to Japan, to their head temple at Mt. Fuji. Rick and I decided to go. I hopped a plane, still anxious about flying but determined to go. I wore my uniform, blue skirt, white top and my new short haircut (cut your hair, cut your karma was the instruction). Japanese members met us at the airport, waving flags and clapping. I felt like a rock star. They were happy to see American people practicing Buddhism. We had the opportunity to stay in individual homes and I found the people to be very sweet. We also stayed at the Olympic Village, where a previous Olympics event was held.

I saw the beautiful Shiraito Falls, the magnificent Mt. Fuji, and also stayed in one of the most elegant hotels I have ever seen, somewhere on the coast overlooking the ocean. I was in awe. My biggest problem on the trip was the food. I had not yet become a connoisseur of sushi so when they served a bowl of soup with little live fish swimming in it, I decided to stick to pickles. They have great pickles in Japan!

The next few years are somewhat of a blur. Too many meetings, too little sleep. I couldn't sit still, even at work, because I went out like a light. Some days it was a challenge to get in a shower and wash one's hair. And when would I get my house clean? I have meetings tonight! I remember one thing though, my biological clock started ticking. I wanted a baby!

Rick and I made another pilgrimage to Japan in 1972 to attend the grand opening of their new big temple, the Sho-Hondo, which had been under construction for years. It was quite beautiful. (Years later, the priests tore it down after a major split between the priesthood and the laymen's organization.) I planned to chant to the original scroll, (actually this one was a big block of wood) for a baby. Rick was not completely on board with my plan.

I encountered a very difficult situation while in Japan. After we arrived at the temple at Mt. Fuji, one of my senior leaders took me aside. They received a phone call from my mother. Dad had a major heart attack and was in the hospital. They didn't know if he would make it. I needed to come home. My leader said, "No. Have faith. Stay here and chant for him." That was a hard one. What if he died and I hadn't bothered to come home? Ultimately, I followed the guidance. I stayed. I chanted for him. I chanted for a baby. When I returned, I drove straight from the airport to the hospital. I found Dad sitting up in bed, drinking a beer and smoking a cigarette. Hospitals were different in those days. This was my actual proof. I'll keep chanting for a while, I guess.

I'm sure my delay in coming home didn't help my relationship with my mom. She was already upset with me for practicing Buddhism. She expressed this clearly the previous Christmas. Rick and I were very short of money at the time so buying gifts for everyone was not an option. Instead, I worked very hard to make and bottle some jam. I also learned how to make homemade candles. I had a good time doing it and put my heart and soul into it. We celebrated at Larry's house, a rare family event. When Mom opened her gift, she looked at me with that look of hers, and said, "What am I supposed to do with this, thank the Buddha?" I was so upset. I grabbed it out of her hand, ran outside and smashed it in the street. I left. It seems to be my pattern. I don't speak up. I have no voice. When things build up, I explode or run, or both.

I got pregnant shortly after that. It did not go well. I miscarried in the fifth month. The doctor said I carried about two months worth of water but the baby never developed. Was the miscarriage due to sleep deprivation, my body being run down, or the fact that I had pneumonia before discovering I was pregnant and took antibiotics? The doctor said I should wait a while before trying again. No problem. I didn't get pregnant easily. A couple of times, I thought I might be pregnant since my period would be a little late but then I would have a heavy one. Rick, known for embellishing things to make a good story, used to tell people I suffered four or five miscarriages. Did I? Who knows? This much I know, my underlying problem with depression reared its ugly head. But no time for that! No time to mourn your loss. Got to move forward. You are a leader!

22.

Well, time to move again. Rick and I rented a nice house in Toluca Lake. I made more money these days. I left my old employer and now worked for Zenith Insurance as an experienced audit reviewer. However, my struggle with sleep deprivation became more of a problem. I was a hard worker but arrived at work late on several occasions and received a couple of warnings from my boss. I didn't know it yet but I was pregnant! As a result, one morning I did not get up on time. I was so tired. When I arrived at work, late again, I was fired. I felt ashamed and humiliated as this did not line up with my work ethic. I took a moment to regroup, working temporarily for Moveable Feast, delivering lunch to people at their offices. I was so excited when I received the news of my pregnancy. Then I started spotting.

Rick and I decided not to take any chances this time. I quit work and rested. I was determined to hold on to this baby! Rick got a job somewhere. I don't remember the details, but wherever it was we didn't have health insurance. I applied for county benefits, which was a little embarrassing but at least I was able to deliver at UCLA. That was probably a good thing because when Kelli was born, on June 14, 1974, she had idiopathic hypoglycemia. I didn't know the gender of my baby until her birth. I'm not sure if ultrasounds were unavailable in those days or if they merely didn't do them for county patients. Anyway, I was thrilled when they said, "It's a girl!" Then they took her away and didn't bring her back. Later the doctor finally came in and told me, "The baby is jittery".

Kelli stayed in the NICU for 10 days. They wouldn't let me hold her. They wouldn't let me nurse her. I could only stick my hand through the cubbyhole of her incubator to touch her. So I drove back and forth from Toluca Lake to UCLA every day to see her and returned home to pump my breasts every two hours, following her feeding schedule. The routine was exhausting! She weighed only 5 lbs. 6 oz. when she was born and later dropped down to 5 lbs. 2 oz. She looked like she was swimming in her oversized infant diapers.

One day I arrived for my visit with her and the nurse asked me if I wanted to breastfeed her. I replied, "Of course, if it is okay!" How wonderful to hold her! She latched on right away and had no problem nursing at all. That night I got a call from the doctor. He yelled at me for nursing her and wanted to know how I managed to talk the nurse into letting me breastfeed. "The baby is jittery again and won't take her bottle," he said. I don't think he liked me.

Kelli recovered well. Once her body figured out how to make glucose, she had no further issues with hypoglycemia. I was filled with joy the day I took her home, albeit a little scared of being a new mom. We decorated one room as a lovely nursery. Rick painted a giant tree and vines on the walls. I loved staying at home with her. I got a reprieve from some of my Buddhist activities too. Life was good for a few months.

Rick managed to get fired from his job, or quit, who can remember. We had no money to pay the rent. So we gave up our pretty little house in Toluca Lake. We rented a house in Encino. Rick found some kind of work. When Kelli was five months old, I found out I was pregnant again. It wasn't an accident. We already received guidance from Mr. K about having another baby (Rick became very close to him after our Hawaii days). Mr. K encouraged us not to wait; two is better than one (we should at least replace ourselves in the universe) so might as well get it done. " Go home and make a baby." Still, after all of my previous difficulty getting pregnant, it surprised me it happened again so fast.

Some women hate being pregnant but not me. I loved having life within me. I loved feeling the baby move. This baby seemed to be a little bigger because, toward the end of my pregnancy, he smashed my lungs and my bladder at the same time. But it was all good. Andrew was born on August 30, 1975. We called him Andy. Again, I didn't know the sex until his birth, again at UCLA. When he saw him Rick responded, "Look at the b**** on that kid. But he's ugly as blue mud!" He wasn't, of course. But he was bigger than Kelli, almost 8 lbs. And healthy! We had a matched set, a boy and a girl.

My joy didn't last long. When Andy was six weeks old, we moved again. Rick wasn't working, again. The landlord told me, "You've had your baby now you need to go." We didn't have any utilities for the last three days we were there. I did not even have water to wash my baby. Rick snuck out after dark with a big Sparklets bottle and stole water with which to flush our toilet. I also got pneumonia again. The doctor told me I must quit nursing my baby. I'm not sure if the instruction was for my sake or the baby's since I was required to take strong antibiotics. With a heavy heart, I complied.

We moved to another house in North Hollywood where we lived for a couple of months. Since we were late paying the rent two months in a row, the landlord decided to check our references. When he discovered our history he demanded we move out. He even offered to put us up in a motel if we would get out right now. Of course, we could not accept his offer. A month later, I left that house at midnight on a moving truck packed with our stuff, a baby on each knee and no place to go.

A friend bailed us out and offered us the upstairs of a two-story house in Glendale. A couple of guys lived downstairs. Later, the guys moved out and we moved downstairs. We sub-rented the upstairs to a nice young man named Mark.

The Buddhists held a convention in New York in 1976 to celebrate the bicentennial. I attended previous conventions in Seattle and Washington D.C. but this one was special because the senior leaders told Rick to stay home with the kids, "Your wife is going". I loved my kids with all my heart but it sure was nice to have a break. I loved New York in spite of the oppressive humidity in the middle of summer. I will never forget my first experience of the subway. It happened late at night, after one of our activities. We were all wearing our colonial costumes, this year's uniform. This poor drunk sleeping on a seat in the front of the train woke up and stared wild-eyed at all of us. I'm sure he thought he had died and gone somewhere! The look on his face! Ah, a little moment of levity.

I tried to reestablish a relationship with my mom a bit. She still drank excessively so I couldn't leave my kids with her or ask her for any help. I invited her and Dad over for dinner one night. She arrived quite drunk. Why did I expect anything different? She insisted on helping me in the kitchen and managed to cut herself with a butcher knife. I tried to stop her. I could see it coming. Blood everywhere. When we finally sat down to eat Mom passed out with her head in her plate. I picked up both babies, told Dad to take her home, and took the babies upstairs until she left. I didn't want them to see her like that. I decided I wouldn't be inviting Mom over again anytime soon. We managed to stay in that house for about six months before we ran out of money again. Next, we moved to Simi Valley. Full Circle.

My sweet Kelli was a precocious little girl, a social butterfly. I had to keep an eye on her at all times. We went to a gathering at a park one day and I had a full-time job keeping up with her. She wanted to go and meet the people. I would spot her across the way and by the time I got there she was gone, off on a new adventure. Everyone loved little Kelli. I lost her at the beach once as well. I spent a very frantic hour looking for her only to have her show up, happy as a lark as if nothing happened. This girl!

Andy, on the other hand, was a Mama's boy. He always stayed close to me. I never worried about losing him, my cautious one. He was quite a talker as a boy though. He started talking when he turned eighteen months old and didn't stop. I struggled to have a conversation with anyone without constant interruption. That changed in time. I hope I didn't shush him too much.

I always thought, if I couldn't work, Rick would pick up the ball and run with it. Clearly, I was wrong. He was obsessed with his dream of being a successful actor and to him getting a full-time job somehow represented defeat. He seemed to think working a regular job was beneath him. Like living in a tract home in the Valley, he wanted better. He made it very clear to me; I better not mess with his dream. To do that would have been the epitome of evil. So I tried to go back to work but daycare was expensive for two babies and just because Rick didn't work did not mean he was going to stay home and babysit.

I found a way. My first boss at Fremont Indemnity agreed to send me audit work I would do at home. I would work as an independent contractor. So I set up a desk in the back of the living room, turned Sesame Street on the television for the kids, and I worked. This was a great arrangement for about a year until my boss discovered her employees were sending me all the work and then sitting around pretending to be busy. So it all came to an end. It was great for a while though. I provided for my family and still stayed home with my babies.

Again I had to move and had no place to go. I had no alternative this time but to go back to Mom's house. I took my babies. Rick refused to go there and chose to live in his car instead. I gave away or left behind most of my furniture since I had no place to put it all, including my desk. I didn't stay at Mom's house long though, a couple of days. She was drunk all the time. She started screaming and yelling in the middle of the night about what a bum Rick was. I couldn't take it. I called a friend and asked her to come and get me. I grabbed my babies and my box with the scroll in it and started walking down the street in the dark until my friend picked us up. *"I think I'm losing it."*

Rick received strict guidance, "Go get a job! You have to support your family!" He actually did it. I also approached my boss about coming back to work full-time. She not only hired me but also decided to train me out in the field as an auditor. At that time, only men held that position and I received more than one comment about this from clients. One man said, "So they let women do this job now?" I didn't care about that. I wasn't a feminist. I wasn't looking to conquer the world. I loved the work though, balancing the accounts, making sense of things. Except, I sure hated putting my babies in daycare. It broke my heart. I would much rather have stayed home with my babies.

We managed to rent another house in Encino. I guess they didn't do credit checks much in those days. We lived there for about a year and worked on getting our life together. In retrospect, I believe we suffered some deep damage to our relationship during those years. I had moved at least twenty-five times in my life so far. I sensed a deep lack of concern on Rick's part about my wellbeing or the welfare of my children. He only seemed to care about his dream. Oh, and he cared about his position as a Buddhist leader. He loved the adoration of his members. I wasn't considering divorce or anything but I knew I would never be able to rely on Rick. I think I just lost respect for him.

23.

The year is 1978. We bought our first home! It was a beautiful ranch-style house in North Hollywood that was built by Pat Brady, Roy Roger's sidekick. It had a big 36-foot wood-paneled den, which Mr. Brady added on to the house. It had five bedrooms, formal dining room, and lush, green landscaping. Although most of the pretty landscaping was potted plants, which the sellers took with them when they moved out. Oh well.

We almost didn't get the house. After the appraisal came in, the lender wouldn't give us the loan because it didn't appraise high enough. I couldn't believe it! This house was amazing! How could it possibly not be worth what they were asking? Our agent called us a couple of weeks later to say they made a mistake. We could have the house if we still wanted it. What no one told us was all the add-ons were done without a permit. I would find out years later when I tried to sell the house. We bought this house before disclosure laws were enacted. I loved this place while I lived there.

We still held Buddhist meetings at our house. Appointed a headquarters leader by this time, I had responsibility for a couple of hundred people. I wasn't in the highest favor with my leader, Mrs. T, since I refused to go out to activities every night of the week. I cut back to an average of three nights. Someone had to raise my children. She told me I was "weak and stupid". I had "no faith" because I wouldn't go out and chant all night with my members. I stood my ground.

Leadership asked me to be a speaker at a women's meeting and share my testimony with five thousand women. I wrote out my testimony and since it was such a large meeting, it had to be approved by Mrs. T. I talked about some of my struggles in early childhood as well as current struggles trying to be a leader and raise my children. Mrs. T didn't like it. Not dramatic enough she said, so she changed it. She twisted my words, making it sound as if I suffered a lack of love for my children. That was not at all what I wanted to say because it wasn't true! It was a lie! As I recall, I eventually complied with her demands. I allowed myself to be manipulated once again. My mom attended the meeting and became quite upset. She asked me, "What if your children hear of this one day? What will they think?" Mom was right!

I tried to stop by Mom and Dad's house for lunch every week or so when I worked in their area. I spent many years estranged from my family, partly due to my own issues and partly due to Rick's refusal to be around them. Mom was sober now. So I tried to spend time with her. Nana lived with her now because she had suffered a stroke. Nana mostly stayed in her bedroom. One day, Nana came out and confronted me, "I still same, in here," pointing to her heart. She said it over and over. I don't think I made an effort to visit her in her bedroom or talk to her much. I don't think I responded to her that day either. I didn't know what to say. Besides, I was wrapped up in my own life at that point, self-absorbed. I missed an opportunity to reach out to her. Sorry, Nana. I never forgot what she said though. It is true. We are the same person inside even when our bodies get old and frail.

I had another car accident that year. It was my birthday and Rick and I drove to Santa Monica to celebrate with Mr. K and Mrs. T. We ate at a Sushi Bar and Rick drank more than his fair share of sake. We had to drop Mrs. T off at her house so I crawled into the hatchback section of Rick's Datsun 280Z to make room. He had a job leasing cars at the time. The Datsun was a company car. I fell asleep back there so after we dropped off Mrs. T, Rick left me in the hatchback. He proceeded to get on the Santa Monica freeway going the wrong direction. It was raining out. The car spun out and hit the center divider. I woke up gasping for breath. I felt a stabbing pain between my shoulder blades. It was so bad that I couldn't breathe. Rick asked, "Are you okay?" I managed to whisper, "No." He said, "Well then, I guess we're in trouble." The ambulance came and took me away. As they loaded me on the gurney, they explained, "Since it's raining we're going to put a sheet over your head." I guess they didn't want me to think I was dead. They took Rick to jail.

Hours later, our babysitter came to get Rick out of jail and they came to pick me up from the hospital, with kids in tow. I was in a lot of pain but nothing was broken so they let me go home. Rick took one look at me and said, "Don't go all dark on me now, OK?" *Really? Okay. I guess I have never been known for my bubbly personality.*

Unfortunately, totaling the company car didn't fare well for Rick's job. We started the whole jobless cycle again, just when we were doing so well. Rick worked for short periods at the local lumberyard, Home Depot, whatever, and then he would find an excuse to quit or manage to get fired.

I had another difficult encounter with Mrs. T one night at a party. She tried to talk to Rick about getting a job. He'd been drinking and didn't react well. Mrs. T took me aside and told me "This situation is your fault and you will see that someday." I worried about him driving home, between the booze and his anger, and asked him to let me drive. But he replied, "A cowboy never gives up his keys." He drove like a maniac, once stopping only inches from the car in front of us. It scared me to death and I thought I would die that night. I felt caught between a rock of the mandate to follow the senior leader's guidance and the hard place of Rick's anger and wrath. It was my fault because I didn't make him work? How would one do that, exactly? I had no clue.

I started having some strange dreams…dreams that I would hold in my heart and ponder. I dreamt I was with Rick at an amusement park on a rollercoaster ride. We were high in the air, at the top of the track, when the car we were riding in flew off the track and soared through the air. It finally hit the ground and traveled down deeper and deeper, into, and under the ground. It kept going down, and down, and down. Finally, I clawed at the dirt, trying to get air. Suddenly we broke through the dirt and we were in a room with a group of senior leaders. They looked at me, looked at Rick and asked, "Why did you bring her here? She doesn't belong."

I also had a dream in which I watched white clouds up in the sky. All of a sudden, the clouds turned into a man on a white horse. In my dream, I asked, "Is that Jesus?" As if in response to my question, the clouds turned into the Virgin Mary holding Baby Jesus. I asked, "Why am I dreaming of Jesus? I am not even a Christian." Hmmm. I believe there are dreams and then there are dreams. Some dreams are merely that, pizza dreams maybe. But some dreams have a profound effect as if the 'universe' is speaking to you. It may take a while to see it but they leave their mark.

We hosted a leader's meeting at our house one night. I always had my issues with certain aspects of the organization but also found value in the practice in many ways. However that night our current senior leader began a rant, informing us we were lazy and lethargic because our Shakabuku numbers were not good enough. Our sales of the World Tribune (the organization's newspaper) were too low. We must overcome our lethargy and get moving! You never know what effect your words will have on someone. Sometimes words that are intended to motivate become poison darts, which enter the heart and are never forgotten. Years of manipulation and promises not fulfilled had built up in my heart. I was so exhausted from my years of non-stop Buddhist activities! How could I possibly be lethargic?

I became more than a little frustrated with Rick's refusal to work. I talked to Mr. K about it. Rick was close to him so I thought if anyone could help it would be him. Mr. K said, "I will talk to him about it, don't worry." Several weeks later, I attended a leader's meeting in which the leader announced, in front of hundreds of people, they were promoting Rick to the position of Territory Chief. He would be responsible for a thousand members. No one even warned me. It came as quite a shock. I guess it didn't matter that he wouldn't work, wouldn't support his family, as long as he served the organization. In all fairness to Mr. K, I did learn at some point he offered Rick a paid staff position but he refused it. Not his dream. They promoted him anyway though. Favorite music: Abba, Little River Band, Supertramp and Donna Summer. Song of my heart: "**I Still Haven't Found What I'm Looking For**" by U-2.

24.

I got a better job at Allianz Insurance. I made more money but I did have to travel more. They sent me all over the state auditing some of their special accounts, facilities for the developmentally handicapped. These facilities have work programs for the higher functioning people that involve sending them out into the community to perform all different types of work. They were, therefore, very challenging to audit.

I began spending time with another auditor, Ray, who I worked with. We attended various conferences together and sometimes audited large accounts as a team. We had a purely platonic relationship but in time we developed a friendship. And eventually, I developed feelings for him.

It began one day when we filmed a training video for an auditor's conference. I played the role of a secretary, greeting the auditor (Ray) when he arrived at my office.

I decided to play the role as an airhead, hair ratted up high, bra stuffed Dolly Parton style, and chomping on chewing gum. I had fun! After we finished shooting we stayed to watch others shooting their videos. As I stood there, I felt a presence behind me, strong as a magnet, calling me. I turned to see who was there and right behind me stood Ray. Who can explain chemistry? Song of my heart: "**Don't Stand So Close To Me**" by The Police. Did I overcome temptation? Well, I didn't sleep with the guy. Was I innocent? No, my heart was not pure. An emotional affair is every bit as damaging to a marriage as a physical one, especially a marriage that is already struggling.

Ray treated me with respect. He treated me like a woman, not a damaged little girl. We enjoyed actual conversations, never about our attraction though. We never discussed that. Too dangerous. We came close once when I told him I needed to have a hysterectomy. "You can go to hell, Lynn!" he told me, "I can't talk to you right now." Well, that was interesting! Could he be upset because I wouldn't be able to have any more children? He also asked me once if I wanted to meet him in Santa Barbara and get my a** in trouble. He said it jokingly and I ignored the question. If he pushed for an answer, it would have been no. I would not do the same thing I saw my mother and grandmother do.

I struggled with my predicament with Ray for a long time. I knew it was wrong but the feelings would not go away. I felt like a hypocrite. So, I finally sought guidance. I proposed stepping down from my position as a headquarters chief. The senior leader's response shocked me! He said, "Lynn, why don't you just go have an affair? Rick deserves it anyway. But don't resign your position because you will need it when the dust settles." *"What is wrong with this picture? Something is very wrong here!"* I did not have an affair, although Rick would accuse me of it later. I did resign my position, which rocked some worlds. A different senior leader, let's call her Mrs. W, informed me, "If you resign your position, the universe is going to punish you. Within six months, you will have health problems, money problems and be divorced." Well, the divorce was not too difficult to foresee. And I did have to have a hysterectomy within six months. My initial diagnosis was cancer, however, the actual biopsy results from the surgery showed "nothing remarkable." Hmmm, punishment? Or was it the 'curse' Mrs. W spoke over me?

I later discovered that the DES drug, which my mom received during her pregnancy, might have caused some of my health issues. The side effects of the drug on a female child who receives the drug in utero include infertility, which I experienced, miscarriage, which I suffered, and adenocarcinoma, which they said I had. Apparently, it can also cause misdiagnosis of cancer in that the DES daughter can present with cellular changes, which appear to be cancer but are not. Wow, who knew?

I asked Rick for a separation, which rocked his world. I needed some time to sort things out. I didn't want the separation so I could be with Ray. That was not my intent. I just needed to breathe! I was suffocating! Song of my heart: "**Cool Change**" by The Little River Band.

Rick stayed away for a month. He insisted we not tell the children. He told them he was making a movie in Florida. In truth, he lived in his car and/or stayed with 'friends'. He called me a month later and told me he wanted to come home. I relented and said he could come home, but only on one condition, he had to get a job. I would not do this by myself anymore, being the sole breadwinner, raising the kids essentially by myself, taking care of the house and running around to Buddhist meetings all the time. It was too much! He agreed and came home. He got a job. He also insisted upon resigning his position in the organization even though I never suggested that at all. He said he didn't think things were going to work out otherwise.

The following year proved interesting. Rick stayed home more. I stayed home more. We didn't have much to talk about. He attended his AA meetings, court-ordered as a result of another DUI. He still attended his Buddhist meetings and when he did, he usually came home late, after I went to bed. Then he quit work again. I asked him for a divorce. I did not want to live this way any longer. I didn't want to wake up in another twenty years and realize that I had a choice. So in January 1985, Rick moved out. I gave him enough money to pay first and last month's rent on an apartment so he wouldn't live in his car again, at least for two months. After that, it was up to him.

I worried about my children's reaction to the divorce. They were ten and eleven years old. I justified my actions by the fact that Rick was hardly at home anyway. I'd always been pretty much on my own with them. They seemed to be okay though. Well, Andy did ask, "Whose idea was this?" Rick told him we had both agreed. Andy said, "No, I want to know, whose light bulb went on first?" I didn't understand the depth of a child's need to be with both parents, Mom and Dad. Some consequences don't show up for a long time.

I felt sorry for Rick. I knew he felt rejected. I knew he loved our children. I also thought deep down inside he loved me too, in his own way. He told me he wanted to be my hero. But he had a blind spot; he was only willing to do it his way and his way wasn't working. It wasn't about money, not at that point anyway. He just was not there for me. I was neglected, not cared for, unprotected. I lost hope that anything would ever change.

Rick was the person that called me "Butterfly". He bought me pictures of butterflies. He bought me butterfly wall decorations. He later even wrote a book called the Bulldozer and the Butterfly. I think he knew the time had come for this Butterfly to fly. Song of my heart: "**Angel Flying Too Close to The Ground**" by Willie Nelson, Rick's song for me.

(Note: As I write this today, I am strangely emotional. It is as if it all happened today, not thirty-two years ago. It was the end of an era. But as I am driving to pick up my granddaughters from pre-school, I noticed the personalized license plate of the car in front of me: "GIDA JOB". What? Oh, dear Lord. And I hear a song on the radio, "**The Way It Is**", by Bruce Hornsby and the Range". It is a song about the civil rights movement, but I hear the lyrics jump out at me. I am reminded there is no point in second-guessing my decision. Nothing would have ever changed. I would have woken up twenty years later to the same life.

III

TRANSFORMATION

Transformation: Change, alteration, conversion, metamorphosis (Oxford Dictionaries)

25.

I spent the next six months trying to regroup, trying to stabilize my home for my kid's sake. Since I had this big house, I decided to take in a roommate, which helped financially. Unfortunately, her teenage son got out of control and she drank a lot so the arrangement had its drawbacks. It's always something. I hung out with my neighbor, Jacqui, and started drinking a little wine myself.

I dated a few guys but found I wasn't really into it. I never did go out with Ray. He moved up to San Jose and joined the police department. He didn't even say goodbye, just disappeared. Perhaps he was afraid of me, or maybe he just wanted to flirt with a married woman. It's hard to say what goes on in peoples' heads.

In June of that year, I attended a business conference held on the Queen Mary in Long Beach. It lasted five days. My female boss and I shared a room. The conference would become a life-changing event, not because of its content, but because of a man there who took a fancy to me. He was a friend of my boss' friend so the four of us spent a lot of time together. He pursued me the entire time. He seemed interesting but relationships weren't on my mind. Besides, the man was married! Greg was supposed to leave the conference a day early and fly to Chicago, but on the last day, guess who showed up at my breakfast table? He stayed over in the hope of hooking up with me. Well, I will spare you the gory details. After the conference ended, I told Greg I had no intention of having an affair with a married man.

Greg called me from Chicago and asked, "Can I come to see you? I'm leaving my wife." They'd been having problems for years. Greg, although not a particularly handsome man, was very intelligent and we had some kind of chemistry between us. I let him come. He stayed with me for a week. When Greg returned home to San Jose, he moved out and rented an apartment. And so we were off and running. I didn't think of myself as 'the other woman'. I rationalized my actions by telling myself his marriage had already ended. I am not proud of that. Oh, Foolish Girl! Watch out little Butterfly!

We flew back and forth to see each other for several months. Then the most curious thing happened, I received a job offer from an insurance company in the Bay area. I think they heard about me from someone in the Auditor's Association. Anyway, I received an increase in pay and they even paid for my move up there. I rented a little house in Campbell and moved my little family away.

Shortly before I moved, I got a call from Ray. He started to tell me about his many regrets. He planned to move back from San Jose. I cut him off. I told him about my move to San Jose. I had met someone. I didn't want to hear about his regrets at that point. It was too late. I asked him not to tell my boss until I had a chance to give her my notice myself. I certainly didn't want her to hear it from him. Ray must have been angry. When I arrived at the office the following day, I discovered my boss already knew I was leaving and Ray was going to be my replacement. Ah, people.

I felt bad about taking the kids so far away from Rick but again I justified my decision with the fact that he didn't see them much anyway. He didn't want to be "my babysitter." I'm sure our move didn't make him happy but he didn't try to stop me. I was confident that my kids would be better off living in such a nice area, away from the San Fernando Valley. Greg kept his apartment since he had his kids part-time. When his kids weren't with him, he stayed at my place.

26.

A year passed and two things happened. First, my employer declared bankruptcy and I needed to find a new job. Second, Greg asked me to marry him. I got a job with the Chubb Group, an international, multi-line insurance company and received another increase in pay, as well as an opportunity to audit the biggest and best of the high-tech firms in Silicon Valley. It was quite a challenge.

Greg and I held our wedding at the Queen Mary, with all five kids. I became Linda (Lynn) Nellis. We had Keith, 8 years old, Krissy, 6 years old, Linda, 4 years old, Kelli and Andy. We were quite a tribe as all seven of us marched down the aisle. We had a beautiful ceremony in the ship's chapel and a lovely reception with a free fireworks show off the bow of the ship. Mom and Dad kept the kids the first night so Greg and I could have one night of our honeymoon alone. But I must say the honeymoon night seemed somewhat anti-climactic since we'd already been together for a year. We spent the rest of the honeymoon, all seven of us, going to various amusement parks.

Greg and I used to spend our evenings sitting and talking for hours. We had that kind of communication. Things were great in the beginning. We did a lot of family outings such as going to the Santa Cruz Boardwalk, Pier 39, and Chinatown in San Francisco. All the kids had sporting events to attend. And we loved to go camping. We rented a motor home and traveled to Lake Nacimiento in Central California several times. We also camped at Trinity Lake and Lake Shasta. Those were the good times. Of course, we endured a fair amount of bickering among the kids, as kids will do, but they also seemed to like each other.

Little by little, those long conversations between Greg and I were helped along by more and more wine. Like the proverbial frog in the pot of boiling water it just kind of happened. I hardly noticed. What started as a glass or two became an entire evening of drinking almost every night. We bought the big bottles of white wine, Carlo Rossi or the boxes of Almaden. (We were so choosy) That is how we coped with litigation, kids fighting, as well as the challenges of work and a blended family.

Greg continued his legal battles with his ex-wife for a long time. After his divorce, he engaged in a lengthy custody battle. After he eventually won that fight, he decided to go after her for reimbursement of his attorney's fees. That one was a dead-bang loser. Throughout this process, I watched this man, who I thought was so together, spend his evenings pacing the floor and scratching his head like a wild man. I would go into the bedroom and hear him talking to himself in the shower, arguing with his ex-wife. I finally reminded him, "I can hear you in there, you know." Eventually, I came to a point of exhaustion. "No more," I told him, "No more litigation."

The kids were fighting more and more. The Brady Bunch we were not. It seemed to me that Greg took his kids side all the time. He claimed the reason was that my kids were older. My kids were supposed to do chores while his kids skated. He blamed every argument on Kelli or Andy. He bought his girls a $1,000 bedroom set but yelled at me for spending $100 on a desk for my kids. He expected me to attend all of his kid's sporting events but Andy had to find his own transportation to his baseball practice. Greg's kids were in a private school. My kids would to have to pay their own way if they planned to attend college. These issues began to erode our relationship. We started arguing a lot behind closed doors. I insisted my children were not going to be treated as second-class citizens in their own home. I don't think my children were aware of these arguments though. I'm sure they saw the favoritism and thought I did nothing about it.

My kids were growing up and becoming teenagers. They were not perfect people. Kelli would later describe herself as a horrible teenager. She wasn't, at least not any worse than I had been. She made some bad choices though and caused me some grief. Andy had his issues too, some of which I didn't know about and wouldn't discover for many years. But those issues are my kid's stories to tell, or not. So I will leave them alone. In any event, it gave Greg reason to complain. He didn't understand Mama Bear. These are my kids. I love them and we were a package deal.

Greg's kids were with us half the time. The house would fill up and be full of noise and chaos, and then it was quiet and empty. His kids were wild and crazy sometimes. I didn't blame them though. They were young and in the middle of a power struggle. Their mom taught them and expected them to hate their dad and us. None of it was easy.

Things came to a head one summer when Greg wanted to take a vacation to Chicago. He insisted I go with him but my kids were not welcome. Only his kids could go. I refused. I was done. While he was gone, I found a place for my kids and me to live. I packed and we were gone by the time he came back. Indeed, I was running again. But my kids were thrilled to be leaving!

The new arrangement only lasted a few months. At first I wouldn't tell Greg where I was but eventually we worked things out and I packed up my kids and my things and moved back. They were not happy. My poor kids! What was I thinking? How could I subject them to this again? I thought I was doing the right thing.

I agreed to go to counseling with Greg even though I had never been a fan of such things. We tried again to work things out, for a while. We saw a counselor for several months and then Greg insisted we quit. My counselor was digging into my childhood. She wanted to do some inner child work. Greg didn't want to do that. He was emphatic, "I don't want a child for a wife! I want a woman!"

The arguments between Greg and I did not rise to the level of violence but we came close a couple of times. One day we were standing in our bedroom arguing. He suddenly got in my face, screaming with both hands clenched into fists. He yelled, "Hit me, go ahead and hit me!" I'd never hit him and had no intention of doing so. I didn't understand. Then I realized he was baiting me. If I hit him he would have an excuse to hit me back. He wanted to hit me! I turned around and walked away.

During another argument, I walked out of our bedroom and took refuge in the bathroom. Greg came barging in, trying to push the door open. I tried to stop him by putting my foot on the door, pushing against it. Being much stronger than me, he managed to push the door in. In my shock, I started laughing. He said, "Oh, you think that is funny, do you?" Actually, no, not really. That was scary stuff for me.

I spent a year in the dentist's chair due to a raging TMJ condition. Apparently, I was clenching my teeth so much they were full of hairline fractures, which resulted in one root canal after another. My dentist was a Buddhist. I made it clear to him that I no longer practiced and had no interest in hearing about Buddhism. He respected my position and left me alone on the issue but did go on to tell me about a weekend seminar on relationships he'd done. He encouraged me to take the "Women's Weekend" as it was called. They held separate seminars for the men and the women. He wanted to introduce me to his wife. He wanted her to go as well and thought we should go together. And we did. The Weekend was held in Oakland and my dentist's wife, Cindy, and I drove there together. Cindy introduced me to the wonderful music of Enya on the trip. I bought a cassette of Enya's music and it didn't leave my car stereo for months, literally.

The "Women's Weekend" was quite an experience. I wouldn't call it a seminar, or a conference, but it certainly was an experience. The leader was a psychologist who had some pretty definite ideas about how a relationship should work. Women were the managers, the responsible parties, but they must do a relationship on a man's terms. The event was pretty confrontational and sometimes combative, with lots of sleep deprivation thrown in. There were some good points though. I understood when they locked doors when the sessions began, to teach women they really can be on time. I had no problem with that because I tend to be a punctual person. I didn't even mind being told to take a five-minute cold shower, timed by my roommates, just to prove to myself I could do it. I am a disciplined person. The man's misogynistic opinions were a little hard to stomach though. Some things he taught sounded like you could have a great relationship if you were willing to be a good doormat. But I did walk away with one gem, which I have not forgotten: "Never believe what a man says. Always believe what a man does." I also met some beautiful women there including Cindy. We met once a week, as a kind of support group, for a long time. (I lost touch with Cindy in later years and, as I am writing this, I learned that Cindy died about ten years ago. She committed suicide. I am so shocked! I don't even know what to think about that. Whatever her reasons, I guess neither the Weekend nor her Buddhism was enough to see her through. So very sad!)

Greg eventually attended the Men's weekend as well. I don't know what the leader taught the men but Greg seemed to come home even more opinionated and hardheaded than before. I have heard the finale of the men's weekend involves some kind of naked tribal ritual. I'm sure the leader teaches the men to do relationship "on their own terms", which didn't really work for me and ultimately didn't work for Greg either.

27.

My mom died on September 30, 1989. A policeman came knocking on our door to give me the news. The kids had been on the computer for hours, which in those days tied up the telephone line, so my dad had called the police and asked them to go to my house. Her death was sudden, Dad said, and not pretty. He had just had hernia surgery when Mom got sick. He had been trying to take care of her. It was a heart attack. Greg went with me to Los Angeles for the funeral. I thought he wanted to support me but, as it turned out, he was more interested in what we could do in my niece's waterbed than in being there for me. Hmm, another black mark in my soul.

I never expected to be so upset with Mom's death. We had a rocky relationship. I thought I would die if I lost my dad, but Mom, not so much. I was wrong. I cried for a year, alone in my car, in the middle of the night and at just the oddest times. Maybe it was because now there was no hope. I could never have the relationship with her I secretly longed for. She was gone.

It was during this time I was diagnosed with carpal tunnel syndrome. The doctor wanted to do surgery on my right hand. I was in pain so I agreed. It did not go well. Six weeks after the surgery my doctor said I had to go back to work, it was time. My problem was I still couldn't use my hand! My incision was inflamed and hypertrophied. The guy had cut straight up my wrist, which was unnecessary, and if he did the incision that way, it should have been zigzagged. I learned later this guy had previously cut off the wrong leg on a patient. Lovely!

My boss saw my hand and said, "No way, we are sending you to another doctor". I saw a hand specialist who prescribed physical therapy for six months. My hand was still not right so the doctor opted to do a second surgery. Then he sent me back to physical therapy for another six months. By that time I had developed carpal tunnel syndrome in my left hand from overuse. So I had a third surgery and six more months of physical therapy. I could not work the entire time. Well, that's one way to get a vacation. Except Greg wasn't having it. He had left his employment to start his own audit company and/or medical billing company and wanted me to work for him when I recovered. He would be the boss. I would be the auditor. I would do the work. He would tell me what to do. While I was recovering he expected me to write his software manual for the medical billing business. Why should I be idle? Never mind the fact I had a cast on my hand. I'm sure it didn't cause too much of a setback in my recovery.

That summer Greg insisted I send my kids to Los Angeles to be with their dad for at least two weeks. It wasn't fair, he claimed, we had my kids all the time! I called Rick and asked him if he could come and get the kids as we were in crisis mode. He came and got them but called me after only one week saying he couldn't keep them. Could he bring them back? He was sorry.

I continued with my counseling sessions, without Greg. I continued to cry in my car, not just about my mother's death but because I was in my second marriage and it was falling apart! *What is wrong with me?"*

My counselor challenged me one day about my drinking. She asked me to test myself to see if I could cut back. And then see if I could go with no alcohol at all. She also suggested I at least go to some Al-Anon, meetings since I was "the child of an alcoholic." I agreed to try it.

"Good grief! I am becoming my mother! How did I get here?" So just like that, I quit drinking. And I told Greg I needed an alcohol-free environment. He was not happy! "I don't want to give up my wine," he replied. Eventually, he agreed but he had a request of his own. He wanted me to go to church with him! I had quit practicing Buddhism by this time but I had no interest in church or any organized religion! "You don't understand," I said, "I am not a church kind of girl!" It had taken several years for me to quit chanting even after I left the organization. I had a hard time sorting things out. *"What do I believe and what had others put in my mind?"* It was a process, a type of deprogramming, I guess.

I tried to separate my feelings toward the organization from whatever value I had found in the actual practice of Buddhism. I concluded the practice was also a disappointment. It did not deliver what it had promised. It was what the Bible describes as "clouds with no rain". I felt the required ritual, the chanting and recitation of Buddhist sutras every single morning and evening, was bondage. And I no longer believed if I didn't do it "the universe" would punish me. I realized I was still doing it out of fear. And the fear left me.

One thing I was clear about though: I had no use for organized religion! Greg explained that we needed "something", a spiritual foundation in our relationship, otherwise he didn't see how we would make it. I relented but did not anticipate finding anything good in a church.

Greg took me to a church in South San Jose where a friend of his attended. I walked in and started to cry. I don't know why but I felt as if I was finally home. The pastor talked about John 3:16, that God loved me, so much he gave His Son for me. I was amazed that I remembered this verse from my Vacation Bible School days. Greg didn't think it was such a big deal as "it's a very famous verse." Not to me though. I didn't know much about the Bible or God, except, when I was little, Mom told me God knew how many hairs I had on my head. That was the extent of my knowledge of the Bible.

After attending a few Al-Anon meetings, I had a very interesting experience. I was trying, for the umpteenth time, to quit smoking. I mentioned it one night in a meeting. I had quit before but every time felt like I was missing my right arm. Seeing people smoking on the street made me jealous! *"Why do they get to smoke, and I can't?"* It was sick! The leader of the meeting approached me afterward and encouraged me, "If you want to quit smoking why don't you ask God for a gift? You know gifts are given, not earned." I thought that sounded good, why not try it. So I did. I prayed, "God if you are real, will you take this thing from me?" I never smoked another cigarette and had no cravings. It was as if I had never smoked! The desire for cigarettes was just gone from me. Truly it was a gift!

I remembered my mom. She was a heavy drinker her entire life until the last twelve years. Then she quit cold turkey. She told me she thought she was dying one night and promised God if He let her live she would never drink again. And she didn't. She and my dad converted to Catholicism, which was surprising since Dad was born in Georgia. A good old Southern Baptist boy, he was. Looking back now, I realize my mom was the best role model I could have had. She showed me the only way to fix a broken life is with God. So I kept on praying and studied my Bible, excited about my new journey.

Around this time I had another powerful dream. I dreamt I was walking in a jet bridge from the terminal to board an airplane. The jet bridge was a circular, tube-like structure, rather than the square ones they have today. Suddenly, the tube started to close in on me. I looked around and saw no one was in there with me. I was alone. The structure kept closing in on me until it was pressing against my body. Then, as I was being crushed, I was no longer in the tube but on the ground below. I could hear screaming coming from inside the tube and looked up to see blood dripping from the seams and out the bottom. But I wasn't in there! I stood on the ground below, in perfect peace. As I awoke, I felt God speak two things. One, you need not fear death; it is just like this dream. One minute you are here and the next you are there. Two, this is what it is like to walk through life with Me. Nothing can harm you. You do not need to fear.

Afterward, I was reading my Bible when a verse just jumped out at me, as if in further explanation of my dream. It was John 16:33, which says, " These things I have spoken to you, that in Me you may have peace. In the world, you will have tribulation, but be of good cheer, I have overcome the world". In my Bible, the footnote to this verse described tribulation as pressure, oppression. It is the same word that is used for **crushing grapes or olives**. This is one of many verses that became inscribed on my heart, never to be forgotten. Whereas Buddhism gave me false promises of "anything I want, physically, spiritually or materially, God gave me an honest, realistic expectation of this life. And He promised to be with me in it.

28.

Greg and I went to church in South San Jose for a year and a half. I wanted to get more involved, maybe join a small woman's group. I was hungry for more. So we found a nice church closer to home. The Home Church was just a few miles away. I loved this place! The music was great! It was alive! And the pastor's messages were so interesting. I was learning and growing.

Just a few weeks after coming to the Home Church, I heard they were having a women's retreat, an entire weekend away in Watsonville. They said, "Come, spend time with God." That sounded great! I went even though I knew no one at this church yet. They held the retreat at an exquisite place in the hills, north of Monterey. I was so excited to be there and looked forward to taking part in the worship and hearing the teachings. I had a surprise coming.

The first night of the retreat, the speaker taught from the book of Ezekiel, chapter 44, which said the priests who had practiced idolatry would be allowed to serve in the outer courts, to serve the people, but would never be allowed to see the face of God. *"What? Oh no, I'm in trouble. What about all those years of practicing Buddhism? I could not undo them! I would never see God's face!"*

This teaching was very personal to me and I took it literally. Until this point, I don't think I had dealt with my involvement with Buddhism. I hadn't even acknowledged it. I had no comprehension of the seriousness of my actions. Now, I realized what I had done: it was spiritual adultery, an affront to God. Just like those Jewish priests, I had served other gods. I was heartbroken! I spent all day Saturday in the meetings, just going through the motions, hurting deeply. On Sunday morning, we worshiped for an hour. Tearfully, I worshiped. Then we walked in silence to an outdoor amphitheater where we were going to take communion. They told us to sit on the bleachers, which were built into the mountain, in silence and prepare our hearts. There was a fire pit at the bottom with cushions set up around it and communion waiting. When we felt ready we were to go to this makeshift altar and take the communion elements individually.

As I knelt on the cushion, I felt hopeless. There was nothing I could do to change my past. I couldn't take back all of the years of chanting or any of the encouragement to other people to do the same. I couldn't unburn the incense, remove the fruit and put out the candles. So I would never be good enough to see God's face.

Then something happened. I felt the presence of Jesus wiping away the tears from my face. Then it was as if he was washing my whole body. And I noticed He was washing me with His blood. I held my heart in my hands and extended it out to Him. He took my heart in His hands and washed it with His blood. Then, somehow, He was transfusing His blood into my heart. I felt a tremendous power surge through my entire body, energy so powerful I almost couldn't take it. And then it was over.

Jesus was not there in the flesh, of course, but He was every bit as real. I didn't understand this experience but I knew without a doubt it was real. In my state of mind, I never could have imagined it. Even in a good state of mind, I could not have imagined the details of this vision or whatever it was. I didn't even know such a thing was possible. But I knew this: I am His and He is mine. I belong to Him. I guess you could call this repentance. It taught me the meaning of the grace and mercy of God. And I felt joy!

After the communion ceremony, we went back to the meeting hall for a final message. This speaker talked of the love of Jesus and referred to another passage in Ezekiel 36:26. This verse became my lifelong promise from God. "I will give you a new heart and put a new spirit within you; I will take the heart of stone out of your flesh and give you a heart of flesh." *"Is that what He just did?"* He would continue to do this for the rest of my life. It is a process. I have not told many people about this experience. They would think I was crazy, one of those radicals! What kind of drugs is she on? But, it changed my life. God manifested himself to me and now I can never doubt He is real. He is with me and He is for me.

"What can wash away my sin?

Nothing but the blood of Jesus.

What can make me whole again?

Nothing but the blood of Jesus."

I continued at the Home Church. I joined a women's Bible study. The worship leader even asked me if I wanted to be on the worship team. Music was always important to me but worship music touched a whole new part of my life, my heart of worship. I decided to get baptized, even though I was baptized as a child. It was important to make this public commitment, especially since I had gone through a conversion ceremony when I joined Buddhism.

Greg was not so pleased with our new church. People raised their hands in the air when they worshiped. He wasn't comfortable with that. I saw him try it one time but I guess it didn't suit him. He was not thrilled with my new excitement or with my involvement in the church. After a while, he stopped coming to church entirely. He used Kelli as an excuse. She had moved out to a friend's house as soon as she turned eighteen. Then she encountered problems and wanted to move back home. Greg allowed her to do so but only on the condition that she attend community college and she go to church for three months. She did both. And she loved the Home Church too. Then Greg announced he didn't want to go to church with Kelli. But she should go so he would stay home. Kelli got baptized and invited Greg to come. He told us he would but he didn't show up. He told me later he didn't come because he thought Kelli was "not worthy" to be baptized, another black mark on my soul. I didn't tell Kelli what he said but just the fact he didn't show up, I'm sure, put a black mark on her soul too. I don't think Greg understood the meaning of baptism. None of us are worthy.

29.

In December 1993, I arrived home from work one day to find a note from Greg. He had taken his daughter, Linda, to a hotel. His friend, Scott, arrived shortly after and explained that Kelli and Linda had a fight. Kelli yelled at Linda for playing the piano while she was watching television. Greg decided Linda was in danger for her life so he took her to a hotel. Scott informed me that I needed to get Kelli out of the house immediately and when I had done so, let Greg know and he would come home. I could not believe what I was hearing! Things had been escalating between Greg and Kelli for a while but this was ridiculous! I told Scott, "Think about it…Kelli yelled at Linda for playing the piano, so Linda's life is in danger? I am not kicking my daughter out on the street, especially not a week before Christmas. Please tell Greg to enjoy the hotel."

Greg came home a few days later, after his custody time with Linda was over. I packed up my kids and we went to Los Angeles for Christmas with my dad. Greg was not invited.

I was shocked when I saw Dad. His eyes were so jaundiced! He said he had been sick and was going to the doctor. We had a nice Christmas together and then I headed back home. Dad told me he should have news back from the doctor soon. I had no sooner arrived home than I got a call. The news was not good, hepatitis C. I got Kelli settled in an apartment with some girlfriends, away from Greg, and headed back to Los Angeles to be with my dad. I didn't want him to be sick and all alone. He needed care. I arrived in early January and learned: no, it was not hepatitis. Dad had pancreatic cancer, inoperable. So I stayed.

On January 17, 1994, those of us in the Los Angeles area experienced the Northridge earthquake. I arrived just in time. Dad lived in Sun Valley, near the epicenter. I woke up in the morning, at 3:00 a.m. to the now somewhat familiar still small voice, "My daughter, I'm calling you to prayer." I thought God wanted me to pray for my dad, so I did and then fell back to sleep. "My daughter, I'm calling you to prayer. My daughter, I'm calling you to prayer." I sat up and tried again. Then, I went to sleep. At 4:30 a.m., the world started to shake and shake and shake. I couldn't get out of bed. There was broken glass all over the house, which Dad stepped in trying to get to me. I have always felt I missed the mark with God's call to prayer that morning but then how was I to know what was coming? Next time I will be more attentive, I hope.

This was not my first earthquake. I was in the path of wrath in 1971, the Sylmar earthquake. Rick and I lived above the Cahuenga Pass. It tore off our oven door and moved our roof over about a half-inch. I was also just five miles from the epicenter in the Loma Prieta earthquake in San Jose. I had just stepped out of an Olympic size pool used for physical therapy. The only person still in the pool when it hit was a lady who had a debilitating muscular disease. She could only walk when she was in the water. This poor lady was holding on to the side of the pool for dear life after the shaking started. The water became a giant tidal wave that sloshed from one end of the pool to the other, even leaving watermarks on the high, vaulted ceiling. A staff member came running out to help this lady, but between the time she jumped in the pool and the time she landed, the water disappeared from that end of the pool. They had to take her out on a stretcher. I have always joked about how people pay me not to move to their neighborhood. Such is my luck with earthquakes.

Dad's house did not suffer terrible damage, as many did. My biggest concern was Dad was scheduled for surgery on January 24th. They couldn't remove the tumor but they were going to create a bypass around it so he could get some liver function because by this time the poor man was itching to death. The aftershocks from this earthquake were intense! Out of nowhere, the house shook, again and again. I feared we would have another big one during his surgery. But the surgery went well. And Dad at least got some relief.

My dad lived until March 30th. I had precious time with him during those months. We talked, although not as much as I would have liked. I didn't want to exhaust him. He told me he suspected Mom had been molested but she never talked about it. She had mentioned to him something strange had happened in the toilet once. There was no further explanation. He said he and my mom loved each other. That's why they hurt each other so much. He told me I was loved.

I took care of Dad as best I could and had help from a hospice nurse a couple of times a week. I tried to make sure he was comfortable. It was hard to tell because Dad didn't complain much. I hope that means we kept him pain-free. During his last week I sat on his bed swabbing his mouth to keep it moist. He had lost a lot of his salivary glands in previous chemotherapy treatment. It was heartbreaking to see him that way but I felt my dad showed such courage in his battle. In a sense, he showed me how to die.

I also had Dad's friend, Sister Lourdes, there to help me. She was there with me when he died and held his jaw shut so it wouldn't have to be broken later after rigor mortis set in. Who knew they did such things? He passed peacefully. So much so I had to watch him for a long time, waiting for his final breath. After his memorial service, a friend of Dad's from his church came up to me and told me that just before she received the news of my father's passing she had a dream of him. He was leaving the church, dressed in a white robe with a big smile and was waving at everyone. He told the people, "I love you and will miss you, but I have to go now." Then he stepped into a limousine that was waiting for him in front of the church. I was amazed at how peaceful I felt at my dad's service. God blessed me with the peace that passes all understanding. Song of my heart: "*I Will Be Free,*" by Cindy Morgan, which I heard in the car during the funeral procession. See you later, Dad. I love you!

30.

Greg supported my stay with my dad at first. After a couple of weeks though, he called me and insisted I come back home where I belonged. He told me I should just take my dad and drop him off with one of my brothers. Let them take care of him. Never mind that they both work. (I was not working at the time). Never mind that neither one of them had a clue of how to be a caretaker. I refused. My brothers could not take care of my dad and Dad only wanted to die at home, not in a hospital. I wanted to give him his last desire.

By mid-February, Greg was even unhappier with my absence. He demanded I come home. Then, he burned up the engine in his car. He forgot to put water in it, I guess. He called and informed me I had to bring my car back to San Jose immediately. That car was intended for work…and I wasn't working. After much prayer and deliberation, I wrote him a letter to notify him, not only was I not bringing the car back, I was not coming back at all. The letter was my attorney's suggestion, to establish the legal date of separation.

I called Andy first to warn him and ask him to please get out of the house. He could fly to Los Angeles. Andy said, "No, I'm fine. Greg is being actually being really nice to me right now. He said he is going to buy me a car." It never happened. I knew it wouldn't. Andy moved to Los Angeles a few months later and lived with me. Kelli moved down and lived with her dad and his new wife.

Greg agreed to stay away from the house one weekend so I could drive up and get my things. My brother Steve came with me to help and to drive the rental truck back. Upon my return, I found my personal things in a pile in the middle of the garage, including all my clothing. Nice! Some things were missing though, such as my record albums, including the autographed album from my Hearts and Flowers friend. My journal, which I kept when I was in my tumultuous teenage years, was gone forever. I left my bed for Greg, despite his behavior. I didn't want it and I had my dad's bed anyway.

How did I justify this divorce? I was a Christian now. I knew what the Bible said. I did not have Biblical grounds. He didn't cheat, that I know about anyway Well, there was the phone call I received from the video store about his overdue videos. Is watching porn considered cheating? It sure felt like it when I got that call. Maybe I never belonged there anyway. The marriage did not start with a great foundation. Maybe it was doomed from the beginning. In any event, I didn't spend much time rationalizing this time.

I knew I couldn't go back. I did not believe I could ever have a close relationship with my kids if I stayed with him and I would not give up my relationship with my kids. He had messed with Mama Bear too many times. He told me, "I know you love me". "No, I don't think I do anymore," I replied, " You took a sledgehammer to my love." Later that year, when he asked me to file for divorce, I filed. I became Linda Layton again.

31.

I spent the next six months living in Dad's house, in shock, numb. Not only had I lost my dad but I also had another failed marriage. I was still on disability due to my hand surgeries. The doctor told me I could not return to my work as an auditor. I did not know how I was going to support myself. There was no way I would ask Greg for spousal support. I told him he could keep the house in San Jose since he had paid a large down payment on it using his separate property funds. I'm sure I was entitled to some of the equity but I didn't want to fight. In return, I asked him to take the credit card debt. I also kept my 401k. It seemed like a fair deal. It was probably more than fair because he accepted the offer. I never spoke to him again.

Sister Lourdes, my dad's friend, had become my friend. That summer, she invited me to travel to Guadalajara, Mexico with her and visit her family. I liked her and needed refreshment, so I went. We were quite a pair! She was a tiny little thing, a nun from Mexico, and there was me, the taller blond from the Valley. Her family called us "Gringita and Nunchita" and asked how we ever became friends. I think she liked having a friend who wasn't Catholic. She could just be herself with me rather than a spiritual authority.

I loved Mexico. Sister Lourdes took me to visit her family in Puerto Vallarta. They were wealthy. I enjoyed staying in their beautiful home. They took me horseback riding up in the hills. And in the shower of this mansion, I saw the biggest cockroach I had ever seen! La Cucaracha! Her family members were warm and lovely people.

She took me to visit her cousins in the small mountain town of Manzanilla, (not the touristy port town of Manzanillo). They were not at all wealthy. I saw how they lived. I saw her cousin sweeping the dirt floor of her house with great care. While we were there Sister Lourdes told me that the next morning I had to get up early because we were going to Pajarete, a morning party in the barn. Pajarete is also the name of the morning drink that is served at the party. They use milk taken fresh from the cow, add a white liquor, cocoa, and sugar. She insisted this was their tradition. I must take part or risk offending her family! So I got up early the next morning and walked with her up to the farm. I watched as they milked the cow directly into an old coffee can, (which I sincerely hoped they had washed) added the other ingredients and told me to drink. Reluctantly, I drank. It was fantastic! However, I noticed only a few people came to participate. They had played a trick on me, stupid Gringita! We went back the following day for the same ritual, only this time many townsfolk came walking up the path to the barn. News had traveled, the Grengita actually drank the Pajarete and they were ashamed. And they were carrying rolls of toilet paper! Pajarete gives you the runs! They were such sweet people. I didn't mind their joke.

As Sister Lourdes and I walked back down the path, we heard a strange sound behind us. Oh no, a very large bull was running loose and was not happy with our presence. He chased us. We ran to a fence just tall enough for us to jump up on, away from the bull. He stopped and stood there staring at us, one foot pawing the ground. It was the proverbial Mexican standoff. One of the Pajarete folks drove down the dirt road in his pick-up truck. He saw us and motioned us to get inside. We ran and jumped inside, escaping from danger just in a nick of time. Whew! I love Mexico!

Next, we stayed with her sister in Guadalajara where I met more of her family. I ate great, authentic Mexican food, listened to mariachi bands and enjoyed the beautiful people. I cried when it was time to go home. They played the song "Guadalajara" for me as I left, which made me cry even more.

While staying with Sister Lourdes' sister, I noticed a singer on the television, performing in a concert. I fell in love with him. His music was so very exciting! I asked if anyone knew who he was but no one did. I thought it was strange as I assumed he must be Mexican. As I waited in the airport café for my plane, I looked up at the television and guess who was on, my new favorite singer! It was a PBS show and the singer was Yanni, Live at the Acropolis. Yanni was Greek, not Mexican after all. I took down the 800 number and ordered a CD for myself and one for my new friends in Guadalajara.

32.

Dad had made me executrix of his estate. Six months later, my brother, Larry reminded me, I was supposed to be selling Dad's house. It hadn't even occurred to me because I was so lost. So I sold the house and found a lovely penthouse apartment in Valley Village. Andy and I moved again.

Selling my parent's house meant going through years of their belongings, giving away important mementos, and getting rid of other things. It was bittersweet. In the process, I found many things Mom had written in her Bible. She wrote many prayers for me and my children, praying we would come to know God. I found an old copy of a Buddhist newspaper, the World Tribune. I must have given it to her at some point. She wrote in the margin, "I may not be much but I belong to Jesus Christ! This is not the truth!" She didn't live to see her prayers for me come to fruition, but her prayers were answered. Her God was faithful. I also found a painting, which had fallen behind my dad's bed. It was a picture of a man ascending to heaven, surrounded by angels. God likes to send me little messages.

I attended a weekend conference called Cleansing Streams. It was a healing ministry. I received prayer about my past, especially about my relationships. During the conference, God spoke to me about my name. I heard, "You know, it wasn't just your parents who named you Linda. I gave you that name." So it was, I was no longer known as Lynn, except to my former Buddhists friends and Rick, who always called me Lynn.

Life was soon to take another unexpected turn. Larry approached me about my future. He said, "Linda, you are trying to figure out what to do with your life, well I am opening a law school, why don't you try it?" "But Larry," I said, "I have no college credits." He explained that I did not have to go to college. There were college-level equivalency exams available that were designed for people like me, people who had lots of life experience. There were books I could buy to prepare for the exams. Wow!

I was forty-seven years old. *"Who starts law school at my age? Well, some people do, I guess. Besides, my kids are grown. I am single. I have no other responsibilities. Why not? What do I have to lose?"*

The next six weeks were consumed with studying English, Math, History, and Sociology. I studied twelve hours a day and received tutoring from Larry's daughter, BJ, who was a high school math teacher. I hadn't seen Algebra since high school. Six weeks later, I went to take the exams and then drove directly to Acton to attend my first Introduction to Law class. Do not pass 'Go' (Monopoly reference), drive straight to law school. It was my long-lost dream.

I spent the next three and a half years in law school. I loved it. Larry spoon-fed me the law. He taught me how to think like a lawyer, how to be analytical. He taught me how to write bar problems, how to pass the "Baby Bar", otherwise known as the First Year Bar Exam, and then the Bar Exam itself. In exchange, I worked for him in his office. What a difference it makes to be in school because you choose to be there. It was exciting to learn!

I passed the bar exam on my first try but not without some drama. The Committee of Bar Examiners granted me extra time due to my carpal tunnel condition and allowed me to bring in an ice chest so I could stop and ice my right hand when needed. Kelli gave me magnet bracelets to wear, which reduced inflammation. They worked amazingly well too. Thank you, Kelli! On the second day, halfway through the multiple-choice exam, I realized I was too far behind. I had forgotten to time myself as Larry had taught me and would never be able to finish! And I understood then why people have committed suicide because of this exam. It was brutal! I felt like throwing myself out the window! Then I heard that still, small voice telling me to take a breath. "Finish all the short problems first, then go to the medium length problems and then tackle the longest ones." Somehow, I got through them all. On the last couple of questions, which were an entire page long, I only had time to read the last sentence, known in law school as the call of the question, and based on the call, I guessed at the answers. Months later I received my results. I passed! More about that later.

I wanted to find a new church after my dad died, so I started attending Church on the Way, which was very famous. I attended there for six months but found it was just too big for me. It was too difficult to meet anyone or make any friends. I was very lonely. Someone told me about a small church that met at the Beverly Garland Hotel in North Hollywood. They rented a room there on Sundays. The membership was only thirty people, nice and small. I became very involved there over the next few years. They invited me to sing on the worship team, which I had missed since leaving the Home Church. I wasn't the best soloist, although I did some of that. Usually, I loved to sing harmony. The pastor also asked me to keep the books for the church, specifically the receivables, not the payables. I continued on my path, learning more about God and what it meant to be a Christian.

Several years later, Pastor had a guest come to preach while he was away. This lady was praying for me after the service when she stopped and said, "The Lord is going to lead you out of this place. Don't tell your pastor though, he would probably faint." I thought it was strange but something inside me knew it was true. I had experienced several disappointments there recently, as when I accidentally learned other members of the worship team were being given a "love gift" for their service but I was not. The pastor previously told me the church could not afford to pay me for keeping the books, so it surprised me they could afford to pay others. Not that I was looking for money. It wasn't about that. I was just surprised Pastor did that. I wasn't looking to leave the church, though. It had helped me through troubled times and I had friends there. So, I put this "prophesy" on the shelf and left it to God. If it were His plan to take me out of there, He would show me.

Another incident occurred a few months later. I had been leading worship on Wednesday nights for a small group when a new guy showed up at church. He played the keyboard. The pastor decided this guy, whom he didn't even know, was going to lead worship instead of me. He announced it at a leader's meeting, without even telling me first. I wouldn't have minded someone else taking over but I was hurt that he didn't bother to tell me first. God spoke and said, "It's time." *"What?"* Wait, I still wasn't ready to leave. Besides, where would I go? Maybe I was just overreacting because he hurt my feelings.

I took a road trip to be alone with God. I wanted to be sure I was hearing from Him, not the voice of my hurt feelings. It was school break so the timing was good. A friend told me one could stay at Catholic retreat houses as an individual retreatant and you didn't even have to be Catholic. I thought this would be a safe way to travel as a single woman. My first stop was the Santa Barbara Mission. Upon check-in, they took me to my room, which was small and simple, located in a beautiful courtyard behind the Mission. Visitors would never know this lovely area was there since they were not allowed beyond the front grounds. And God spoke something to me that would become the theme of my time with Him on this trip, "The view is different on the other side."

I spent several days there enjoying the Mission and the nearby beach. Then I drove up north to my old stomping grounds, the Santa Cruz Mountains. There was a Catholic retreat up there, nestled in the mountains. It was so lovely. I had a private cabin and had access to the main dining room for three home-cooked meals a day. I continued in prayer, asking God for direction. One day I found a path that led down the hill to a deserted area in which there was a quiet stream. I sat by the side of the stream for a while, just thinking and enjoying the environment. Then I felt the strongest prompting, "Cross over to the other side." I replied, "Lord, they blocked it off with tape that says, 'Do Not Enter'." "But no," He said, "I want you to cross over to the other side." So I did. The stream was shallow so crossing was not a problem. On the other side, I turned around and saw the view was completely different on the other side! *"Hmm. Are you trying to tell me something?"*

I stayed five days and then took the coastal route back down Highway 1, instead of taking Highway 101. It took longer but I wasn't in a hurry. My next stop was Morro Bay. I had been there many times before when I was married to Greg. It was one of my favorite spots, with the huge rock mounted out in the water. After I arrived, I walked out along the left side of the rock as I had always done. It was a very rocky stretch and you had to be careful climbing on the rocks. Suddenly I heard God say, "Go to the other side." It baffled me, "What other side? I didn't know there was another side." Well, I found a tiny dirt road leading to the other side of Morro Rock. And on the other side was the loveliest beach I have ever seen. It was so flat and stretched for miles. You could walk far out into the water before it became deep. God said, "The view is different on the other side!"

I decided to trust God. I left the church and started yet another new journey. The pastor was not happy when I told him. He even prayed over me and said, "Linda, God did not tell you this. The Holy Spirit is telling me right now, it was not Him." He prayed, "Tell her right now, God, let her feel your Holy Spirit, right now." I felt nothing and knew I had to trust what I heard for myself. I wasn't angry with the pastor and still loved him. But I had to listen to God, not man.

33.

Andy and I stayed in the Valley Village apartment for a year and then the landlord raised my rent. I decided to move to an apartment in Reseda. Andy, who now went by Drew, decided he didn't want to move there with me. He was in community college and had a girlfriend, Melinda. They moved in together. So, I moved to Reseda and lived there by myself for a while. I didn't feel very comfortable there. There was a lot of crime in the area. And I wasn't used to living alone.

I had some money saved from my father's estate and also from my worker's compensation settlement. So I bought a small condo in Palmdale, nothing fancy. It was closer to the law school in Acton. How many times have I moved in my life?

After moving to Palmdale, I looked for a new church. I tried several different places, including the Highlands Church. I heard their singles group was having a New Years Eve party along with the singles group from the Vineyard in Lancaster. It was at a guy's house named Tom. I had made no friends in the Antelope Valley yet, so I went.

Tom had a very nice house in Quartz Hill. He was a retired air force guy who now worked on C130 airplane engines at a company in Mojave. I thought he had his stuff together and not bad looking either. He was a Christian, too. I even saw him down on his knees one time, worshipping God. And he was such a charmer, a good old Southern boy. The pursuit began. Watch out Butterfly! There's a spider web in the bushes over there!

Tom and I dated for three months and then we got married. Larry tried to warn me, "You are in your last year of law school. The last thing you need is any distractions! Law school is a jealous lover."

God tried to warn me. When I stopped to pray about this marriage, I heard that familiar voice, only it was not still and it was not small. It screamed. "DON'T DO THIS!" "*Wow,*" I thought, *"That couldn't have been God."* And I continued with my plans. I asked a second time a few weeks later. The same thing happened. But, I went on my own way. Foolish girl! Why didn't you listen? When will you learn?

I married Tom on March 30, 1997. The weather, which had been lovely, turned bitter cold that day. My former pastor married us in the gazebo at Larry's ranch in Acton.

The wind howled through the place so strong I had to put on a black leather jacket over my wedding dress. Larry had plumbing problems that day so it was not very pleasant to go inside the house. I had invited the pastor to conduct the ceremony since I knew no one in the Antelope Valley yet. The pastor's wife commented, "Why has the weather turned on this wedding?" "*Hmm, let's not go there.*"

Before the ceremony, I heard Tom on a rant, screaming at one of his sons, Jason, at the top of his lungs, which was alarming. But…I went ahead with my plans. My name became Linda Deal.

Tom and I left for a two-week honeymoon, one week on the central coast and then to Rosarito Beach in Mexico. I hadn't slept with him before the wedding since I was a Christian now. Uh, it was not great! I don't think my thighs were skinny enough for him, or I was not something enough, I'm sure.

When we returned, Tom's son, Tommy, informed him his ex-girlfriend, Judy, had called. She wanted him to call her. I will never forget the look on his face. I think he called her the same day. It took five months to find proof of his affair. He had admitted to talking with her, even that he had gone to see her, but nothing more, he claimed. Then, one weekend, he said he was going away by himself to Solvang, to be alone and think about things. He worked in Upland now and told me he was leaving directly from work. After he came back, I found an ATM receipt from a bank near Judy's house in Lancaster. The confrontation was not pretty.

I suspected that Tom was cheating on me, but I thought, "*I am a Christian now. I cannot divorce again.*" This was my "Christian marriage." Surely, God would turn things around. Besides, I cared about this guy, despite everything that had happened. Don't ask me why. It was as if he had a spell over me.

I considered leaving Tom when I found proof of his affair. The problem was I had leased out my condo for a year. I couldn't go back. I had given away most of my furniture. And money was short. So began a cycle that would continue until I left. Tom would leave and go live with his girlfriend. He said he wanted me to stay at his house. He wanted me to finish law school. We would figure it out. Then he and his girlfriend would have a fight. He would come home begging me for forgiveness. "I was so deceived," he would say. A week later, I would come home to find a note. He was gone again. The last time he did this was only one week before my bar exam. How I managed to study, I don't know. Maybe it was an escape from the torment of my life.

When Tom was home, he was cute, playful and charming. I thought things were changing. He teased me, saying he should get a personalized license plate, which said, "Kept Man." He called me his "Cash Cow." I didn't like the sound of that but at least it sounded like he didn't plan to get a divorce. He also joked once, "Can't all three of us just get along?" Maybe he wanted to have his cake and eat it too. They say variety is the spice of life. And it wouldn't be a bad deal for him if I became an attorney and supported him now would it?

I went away by myself one weekend to a Korean Christian retreat up in the mountains. This place was different. Instead of a room, they gave you a cave-like structure to stay in. "*Cool, I could do a cave right about now.*" I intended to stay for the weekend. I spent one afternoon and then I got a call from Tom asking, "Please come home. The boys have been arrested." They were involved in a drive-by shooting at a Taco Bell in Lancaster. Tommy was driving and Jason was the shooter. Thankfully, he didn't kill anyone but they were both charged with attempted murder and a hate crime since the victims were black. The prosecutor only offered plea deals to the boys as a package deal so both boys had to accept, all or nothing. They both went to prison. Larry represented Tommy and got him a lighter sentence. Tom and I enjoyed some of our best time together going to see the boys in prison. When Tom was otherwise engaged, their mom and I would go. They transferred the boys around a lot so I got to see the inside of several different facilities. I tried my best to encourage Jason and Tommy for as long as Tom and I were together. Then I had to quit. I just couldn't do it anymore.

I stayed at Tom's house until the following summer. Then I finished law school and sat for the Bar exam a week later. I had accelerated my last year of school, finishing a year's worth of work in only two quarters because I needed to finish early and get out of his house. It was insane! I prepared for the Bar exam at the same time and spent months studying twelve hours a day. It was grueling work. I developed strategies for staying alert, such as moving from room to room every couple of hours, or even reading standing up.

As soon as I completed the exam I left Tom's house and went to stay with a friend of mine in the San Diego area. I stayed with her for a month and when my tenants finished out their year's lease, I asked them to vacate my condo. During that month I did nothing. I rested. I took walks. I read my Bible and listened to worship music. And tried to regroup, again.

Before I left for San Diego, we had a small celebration in Santa Barbara, Kelli, Mark, who was a friend from law school, his current girlfriend and I. We ate dinner at a Mexican restaurant on the pier. After dinner and a couple of margaritas, we went down to the beach. It was a warm, beautiful evening and the water was inviting. I was free! No more hours upon hours of studying, writing briefs and memorizing rules of law. I ventured into the ocean wearing my jeans and shirt. Kelli, who is not fond of water, remained on the shore. She became concerned about me and starting yelling, "Come back, Mom! Mom, come back!" But I was fine. I wasn't drunk or suicidal. I was just releasing a tremendous amount of stress. Even a conservative, subdued person like me has to get wild and crazy occasionally, right? You cannot imagine my relief. Whether or not I passed the Bar, I was finally finished with my brutal study routine. And I could move on.

While in Santa Barbara, Kelli introduced me to the music of the wonderful Natalie Merchant. She took me to a music store and bought her CD for me. I listened to and sang her songs for a very long time. Songs like *"Break Your Heart," "Life Is Sweet,"* and, *"Kind & Generous,"* which I sang to God.

No sooner had I moved back to my condo but I got another call from Tom. The police had arrested him. His girlfriend had charged him with rape, kidnapping, and false imprisonment. She claimed he had taken her against her will and kept her at his house. She said he held a gun to her head and demanded sex. I believed none of it. I suspected she didn't want him once I was out of the picture. Go figure.

I went to see Tom in jail and felt so sorry for him. Sitting on a bench with his head hung between his knees, he looked pathetic. (He would later become furious when I told him that. It was a bad choice of words, I guess) A few days later they released him on his own recognizance. Judy had refused to do a rape kit. He claimed to have substantial legal fees and asked me to please give him another chance. And would I please let him move into my condo? That way he could rent out his house and save money to pay off his legal bill. Well, he was still my husband. Maybe God was working on something here.

The next few months were hell. Tom, who was not a happy camper, moved into my condo. Life got even crazier. I had my friend in law school, Mark, a much younger guy and merely a friend. Tom ordered me not to talk to him. He dominated. He controlled. Once he was in my place, he became a nightmare to live with. He got laid off from work and became indignant when I asked him what he intended to do. I was depriving him of his opportunity to collect unemployment! At the same time he tormented me with comments such as, "Boy, wearing this wedding ring is sure cramping my style at the gym," and "You know, Judy had no fat on her thighs." Once, he saw a guy flirting with me and told me, "That's okay, he wouldn't want you after he had you." His comments were poison darts that pierced my heart.

34.

I received the results of the Bar exam in November 1998. It was a long wait, three months of suspense, but I passed! Soon after, Larry received a phone call from an entertainment production company in Valencia. They said they were looking for a law student to review legal documents. Larry called me and suggested I check it out. So I did, explaining I was not a student as I had just passed the Bar, but I was interested in their position. We set an appointment for the following week. Then they called me back and asked me to come the next day instead.

I got my first job as an attorney, with a starting salary of $50,000. As it turned out, the job involved a little more than reviewing legal documents. It involved celebrities and a multi-million dollar lawsuit. The company had just fired their former, very prestigious Beverly Hills law firm. They had twenty-three boxes of legal pleadings from this case, which had been going on for three and a half years already. They also hired another brand new attorney. We would work together and also have access to other experienced legal counsel. If the case went to trial, they would make sure I had help.

Things ended between Tom and me during this time. We were in Pasadena one day, looking at houses to buy when I received a phone call from Mark, my friend from law school, the one Tom had forbidden me to talk to. It enraged him when he found out Mark had called! He drove like a maniac, going 90 miles an hour, all the way home to Palmdale. He screamed at me the entire way, accusing me of all kinds of things, all untrue. Tom kept insisting I confess and everything would be okay. Nothing I said could change his mind. I refused to confess to something I had not done. Maybe he wanted to relieve his own guilt. Who knows. The fight went on late into the evening. He even took off his wedding ring and threw it in the toilet. It was insanity! I went to bed with that old familiar feeling; I didn't care if I died that night. Something inside me just snapped.

I woke up the next morning and knew this could not go on. Maybe his girlfriend, Judy had a case against him after all. This guy was nuts. I would certainly die if I stayed with him. So I went to church by myself, back down in the Valley. I talked to my old pastor about what was going on and I never went home. I just couldn't go back. The pastor found a place for me to hide.

Five months passed before I finally got Tom out of my condo. He wouldn't leave. I went in when I knew he wasn't there to get my clothes. I had the locks changed. He had them changed again. He had locked the filing cabinet so I couldn't get my legal documents, so I took the whole cabinet with me. I asked him for a key. He refused. I told him I would have to break the thing open if he would not give me the key. He replied, "If you do, I will break you open." I got a restraining order. He filed papers with the court to have exclusive use and possession of my condo and posted the notice on the front door. He also asked the court to order me to pay him spousal support. I guess he wasn't happy his Cash Cow had left the barn. His plan had failed.

I came to appreciate the snail's pace of the legal system in Lancaster when the court ordered one continuance after another. Tom could not have his motion heard in court so he could not get an order for spousal support from me. He eventually had to get a job…in Texas! Yeah, love that song, all my exes are in Texas. Not really, Greg moved to New York.

When I finally got my divorce, Tom got nothing from me. He hadn't paid for anything concerning my legal education so no reimbursement was due him. Strike one. I wasn't working during most of our marriage, he was, so no spousal support for him. Strike two. And he had no proof he was entitled to any part of my property, as he claimed. Strike three. And he had to pay me the community property portion of his 401k, which he earned during the marriage. Now, I try to be a benevolent, generous person. Under these circumstances… I took the money.

I never went back to my condo. Instead, I put it on the market and rented an apartment in Valencia, in the Town Center. It was lovely but expensive and quite small. I lived there for a year. I went to work, came home and just sat, looking out at the golf course. There were times I would realize it was 9:00 at night and I was still sitting there in the dark. I think I was trying to process what had happened in my life and where I was going. Marriage #3…down the tubes. I never expected to be married three times. How did this happen? What was it with me and men? The wounds Tom inflicted were deep and raw. Where do I go from here? How will I ever trust anyone again? So many questions, so few answers. I had set myself up for this pain. I didn't listen to God. He would have spared me this. I knew that, but it didn't make it hurt any less.

35.

Thank God for work! The case went on for another year and a half. I experienced just about every kind of legal motion one could encounter in a civil case. I was surrounded by experienced attorneys the entire time. I learned so much. Larry once said, "Any resemblance between law school and taking the Bar exam is merely coincidental. Any resemblance between taking the Bar exam and practicing law is even more coincidental." I think that's true to some extent but, thankfully, Larry did a good job teaching me "where to find what I need when I need it".

I had only worked there a few months when my boss, Vince, fired the other attorney. He wasn't working out. And he increased my salary to $90,000 a year since I would carry a heavier load.

The case involved Gianni Russo, who had played Carlo in "The Godfather." Although I did not represent him, I represented several companies Gianni had created. I also represented his wealthy investors, the Bakrie family, who owned practically half of Indonesia. And I represented the production company that shot Gianni's children show at issue in the case, as well as the film distributor. This was heady stuff for a young, well, not young, but a new attorney. A woman who claimed Gianni had stolen her ideas and breached his contract with her was suing all these companies.

Some of the depositions required traveling to Las Vegas and New York a couple of times. Gianni's insisted his deposition be conducted in Las Vegas, not in California. I have forgotten his excuse. After the deposition concluded, I boarded my plane to return home only to find Gianni sitting in first class. He looked at me and said, "Ah, Linda, my love, come join me in first class." He was obviously on his way back to California but he offered no explanation.

I took Kelli and Drew with me on one of my trips to New York. They played while I worked. We went to Central Park together and we saw "Cats" on Broadway, one of my favorite musicals. Song: *"Memories"* by Betty Buckley.

It was an exciting time. It was especially exciting to discover, in the middle of a deposition, this case involved all kinds of mafia connections. This top mob boss was protecting this person. That mob boss was protecting that person. I heard names like John Gotti, the Gambino Family, and the Genevese Family thrown around like it was no big deal. Whoa! What in the world had I gotten myself into?

By the time we went to trial, Gianni's attorney quit, which was too bad because I had been working closely with him. Gianni asked me to represent him as well since I was representing his companies but Vince said, "No." I had also been working with attorneys for Fox Children's Network (also a defendant) but they were dismissed from the case after opening statements, which left me standing alone! I thought I would throw up on the courtroom floor when the judge announced his ruling: Fox was out! I had never done a trial before as an attorney! And all of the promised help failed to materialize. Vince told me "Linda, you can do it!" I had been successful in getting the investors dismissed as defendants in a Summary Judgment motion, so I guess I was already a hero. I had accomplished the most important goal, the one Vince cared about. So, I had no choice but to put one foot in front of the other and figure this trial thing out as I went.

Not surprisingly, I was pretty green. It was the ultimate lesson in multi-tasking, to learn to listen to testimony, to hear its substance, determine how to bring the cross-examination, listen for objectionable statements and make the appropriate objections in a timely manner, all at the same time. This process becomes second nature as one becomes more experienced but it was stressful for me, flying by the seat of my pants as I was. I went home after court each day and worked late into the night, preparing for the next day. I only had one assistant, unlike my opponent who had an extensive support staff.

The trial went on for six weeks. I enjoyed it, for the most part. I managed to get the production company dismissed as a defendant after the Plaintiff's case-in-chief. Another victory! I tore the Plaintiff apart on cross-examination. I could tell her attorney was getting worried. Her son (also Louie The Dome's son, if you get my drift) started hanging out in the hallways of the courthouse, staring me down every chance he got. The attendant in the parking garage reserved a parking spot for me, close by where he could keep an eye on my car for me.

I could deal with this. It was not my first experience dealing with danger in the workplace. As a worker's compensation field auditor, I had an accountant for a racehorse owner threaten to take out a contract on me after his cajoling and attempts at bribery had failed. I had a real estate agent rip my audit out of my hand and tell me to get out. No harm had come to me then. Still, I was comforted by the fact that my car was being watched.

When I began my case-in-chief, on a Friday, the plaintiff filed a motion to prevent me from bringing evidence on behalf of my main defendant. Their corporate status in Las Vegas had lapsed. I would not be able to have it reinstated before Monday when the judge would rule on their motion. What now? Vince told me not to worry. He would fly there over the weekend. "But Vince," I said, "It takes days to get this process done. It's statutory! It's impossible to do it any quicker and there is no time!" Vince walked into court on Monday morning with a Certificate of Reinstatement in his hand. When I looked at him, my eyes open wide, he said, "Don't ask, Linda." So I didn't.

Overall the trial was going pretty well until Gianni visited California. The plaintiff's attorney caught him here and served him with a subpoena to force him to appear at trial. Gianni had no intention of doing so. I don't know his reasons for refusing to testify, as he wasn't my client, but he failed to appear. The day the judge announced this development to the jury was the day things went downhill.

The jury deliberated for about ten days. While we waited, Vince sent my assistant, her husband and me to Cabo San Lucas for a mini-vacation. It was a little risky since we didn't know how long the jury would be out, but we took a chance. We figured we could always fly back if need be. I didn't drink often after my experience in San Jose. When I did, I only had one drink, two at the most. I drank on this trip, lots of margaritas. We partied! I went scuba diving and got bit by some unseen fish on the butt. We went on the "booze cruise" and I took part in the games, hanging upside down and backward off the back of the boat, loving the ocean spray in my face. I ate amazing ceviche and drank tequila. The trip was a stress-buster.

After we arrived home, we got the call. The jury was back. As I sat in the courtroom, waiting for the jurors to enter, I noticed the plaintiff's counsel was sporting a new goatee. When I commented on it, he responded, "I thought I might as well look the part, devil's advocate." He continued, "Linda, I would sue Jesus Christ himself if he walked the earth today." Chilling!

The jury came back with a multi-million dollar verdict against my defendants. I spoke with several jurors afterward and they told me they were so confused. They did not understand what was going on with this trial, but when the judge told them Gianni was subpoenaed and did not show up, it all made sense. That was it.

I felt terrible, even though I understood there was nothing I could have done. I couldn't force Gianni to come to trial, but I still felt like a failure. It was a David and Goliath situation but David lost. Maybe I was just a lousy lawyer.

Vince was not at all concerned about the loss. The only defendants left in the action when the verdict came down were empty shell corporations, except for one Distribution Company in New York, but no one seemed to care about them. Vince sent me to Jakarta, Indonesia to work for a week for the investors. They were pleased. The judgment had not touched them.

36.

My trip to Indonesia was quite an experience. I spent one night in Singapore, which is the most pristine, beautifully manicured place I have ever seen. I flew the next day to Jakarta, which is the dirtiest. There was trash everywhere. Goats were wandering on the center divider of the roads in the city. I saw all of this as I drove through the city in my luxury car, driven by my private driver back and forth from my most elegant hotel. I will never forget the embankment of flowers leading to the lobby of my hotel. It was spectacular. They took me to the best restaurants and I learned to eat Indonesian style, no utensils, only clean hands. On one of the few occasions I ventured out onto the street alone I realized I had all of this wonderful protection for a reason. The Muslim women on the streets could have killed this blond woman, who was not wearing a burka, with their glares. The streets were probably not safe for me.

After I finished my work in Jakarta, the investors sent me to their privately-owned resort in Bali for the weekend. Another associate from my company was with me for this trip. She and I sat on the beautiful beach in Bali watching the planes land on the airstrip, which hovered over the sand and extended out over the ocean. One of the investors had told me, "Linda, you will love Bali, it is the most spiritual place." The population of the island, unlike Jakarta, is Hindu rather than Muslim. Everywhere I went there were statues of their gods, which looked like demons. Even the poorest-appearing dwellings had these statues in their yards, for their protection I was told. All of the shops had little plates of offerings to their gods on the steps. You had to be careful to step around them when you entered. The people were sweet and kind. I felt such love in my heart for them. But even though it was, in fact, a spiritual place, it felt so dark. I remember wondering *how these beautiful people could be so deceived as to pray to these statues.* But then I had chanted to a piece of paper, hadn't I? So as I lounged under a waterfall in the spectacular eternity pool at the resort, I lifted my arms to God and prayed for these lovely people.

I stayed on at Valencia Entertainment for almost a year after the trial. I was their in-house counsel, handling all of their contracts, and other various legal cases. Vince seemed to have a talent for attracting lawsuits. Vince took the company public, changing the name to ValCom. I worked with the attorneys who handled the process with the SEC and learned a lot, but some things I saw concerned me. I had worked hard for my law license and didn't want to lose it because of any impropriety on someone else's part. So Vince and I parted ways. He would later become embroiled in much litigation with his new company. It is a good thing I left when I did. Vince is gone now. I understand cancer took most of his tongue.

37.

I rented office space and set up shop. I advertised for work as an entertainment attorney since that had been my experience. However not being with a large, prestigious law firm became a disadvantage at that point.

I attended a church conference in Pasadena. A speaker at the conference called for any attorneys in attendance to come forward. *"Attorneys? What the heck?"* I went forward, along with two other attorneys, both male. My dress was casual. Maybe that's why the leader looked at me and asked, "You are an attorney?" "Yes," I replied with a little attitude. Then the man prayed over me and prophesied, telling me I would help many women with domestic violence issues and child custody problems. He took a bottle of olive oil and poured it over my head, anointing me. I wondered if he had typecast me based on my gender, as I had no interest in practicing family law. I had enough personal experience with that stuff.

Well, guess what kind of business walked in my door? Yep, family law cases, including women with domestic violence issues and child custody problems, which I had no interest in. I soon met two ladies who worked as paralegals in family law and had somehow found me. They needed a supervising attorney in order to comply with licensing laws. If I would do that for them they would also send me work. We struck a deal and I began yet another new journey.

I would spend the next fifteen years handling hundreds of family law cases. I saw many families torn apart and child custody tug-of-wars, which broke my heart. I encountered other attorneys who would lie, cheat and steal to win. Some attorneys refused to even talk to me until their client had racked up $10,000 in legal fees. The bailiff escorted me to my car in one case to protect me from my client's crazy ex. I met some beautiful people who I felt honored to help. And I met angry, vengeful people who would never be happy no matter what you accomplished for them.

38.

After living in my rented condo for a year, I decided it was time to purchase something. I liked Valencia. It was so much nicer than the San Fernando Valley. I bought a cute, two-story townhouse on a golf course just south of the Town Center and remodeled it, making it my own.

I found a new church, The Santa Clarita Vineyard. The worship was amazing. Vineyard music was a whole new world for me. It was great. Although, I felt the church was rather big, around 700 people, and it was hard to make friends. So I joined a small group from the church that met once a week in someone's home.

I met a guy in this group named Richard. He was involved in a ministry at a Juvenile Detention Camp, Camp Scudder in Santa Clarita, and ministered to boys there. He suggested I come, that I would like it. It was a Catholic ministry but he said they welcomed all faiths. You didn't have to be Catholic to participate. I had been looking for a ministry opportunity within the church but there didn't seem to be anything for me. Maybe this 'parachurch' activity would be the answer. It was perfect! I loved working with the boys and went one night a week. I had a special place in my heart for teenagers

85

in trouble. We would meet together as a large group and enjoy music and a speaker, and then we would break into groups of five or six so the boys could talk. I was surprised to see how much these boys would open up about their lives. Richard asked me to join their little band and we played there every week. I sang a song that would become one of my favorites, *"**God Is My Refuge**"* by Kate Miner. This led to my joining the worship team at The Vineyard as well, which was such a wonderful experience.

One night we had a foot-washing ceremony. We all brought plastics bins and bottles of water and picked out a few boys to minister to. One of my boys looked at me and said, "No, no way. You are not washing my feet." I told him this was an act of love and service. I wanted to do it. He shook his head, "No". I explained to him, Jesus washed the feet of his disciples and Peter hadn't wanted to let Jesus wash his feet either. He still shook his head, "No!" I said, "Bobby, Jesus wants to wash your feet!" "Okay," he replied, as he took off his dirty old boots. He let me wash those feet. I loved showing him his worth and demonstrating the love God had for him. It was a special night.

There was a girl's probation camp next door, Camp Scott. The leaders of the ministry at the camp invited me to serve there also. They were having a big meeting for the entire camp and asked me to be a speaker. Now we are hitting home. In front of several hundred troubled girls, I began my testimony, "How many of you know, when you go out on the streets alone bad things happen?" Most of them raised their hands. From my heart, I went on to share things of which I rarely spoke.

I continued ministering to the girls at Camp Scott, although here it involved meeting with girls individually. Their stories would tear at my heart and I tried to encourage them as best I could. Eventually, they moved the boys out of Camp Scudder and they used both camps for girls. And after a couple of years, my time at the camps ended.   39.

It was around that time, 2002, I hit another bump in the road. I developed a frozen shoulder and couldn't lift my arm for nine months. I tried everything to ease the pain: physical therapy, chiropractic, acupuncture, and anti-inflammatories. Nothing helped. So I went to Holy Cross Hospital for an outpatient procedure.

After twelve minutes under the general anesthesia, I crashed. I suffered cardiac arrest, respiratory failure, and was posturing from lack of oxygen. They could not finish the surgery since they had to rush me to the cardio lab, trying to keep me alive. I went into tachycardia, then bradycardia and the left ventricle of my heart was ballooning.

My poor children were in the waiting room and heard the Code Blue. Kelli said she knew it was me and dropped to her knees to pray. She later told me a young, Asian girl walked in the room and introduced herself as my anesthesiologist. Kelli said the girl appeared "visibly shaken." The girl said she tried to warn them that I had a rash going up my arm. Poor kids also witnessed me being rushed off to the cardio lab on a gurney. Kelli saw me posturing and knew enough about biology to know it was not a good sign. The posturing indicated severe brain damage.

I woke up five days later. Kelli told me I was conscious after three days but became so agitated when they explained what happened that my blood pressure would go through the roof, so they medicated me to allow me to stabilize. When I finally woke up, I remember thinking, *"Oh, I guess they kept me overnight after all."* I had no memory of anything that happened during those five days.

Since Holy Cross is a Catholic hospital, they left little notes of encouragement on my breakfast tray in the morning. That morning, when I was alert enough to comprehend what had happened, I received a note that said, "The Lord Protects You," and I understood with my whole heart and mind it was Him who kept me alive. The doctors may have kept my body alive but it was God who brought me back.

After I woke I had two visitors. One was a young Asian **male,** who introduced himself as my anesthesiologist. *"What???"* The other was my surgeon. He asked me, "So, what kind of malpractice, I mean practice do you do?" He knew I was an attorney. I thought, *"What is going on here?"* They made an official diagnosis of 'Tsuchihashi Syndrome', which was later renamed 'Takusubo Syndrome'. The name refers to a study done in Japan concerning people who had no history of heart disease who had suffered cardiac arrest based on stress, whether physical or emotional. Some people call it "white coat syndrome." I found this strange as I had previous surgeries and never had a problem with anesthesia, or fear of doctors. Maybe I should. My pre-op had shown I was fine. No one could give me any answers regarding what happened. I didn't know if the doctors had done something wrong and they were covering up or if I had some kind of freak reaction. If it was this syndrome, I was told, it could happen again. So much for the facelift I always thought I would have someday. Maybe it is just as well. I haven't had great luck with my surgeries.

As soon as I was stable, they sent me home, even though I was still in great pain. I still had the original issue with my shoulder since they could not complete the surgery. And now I also had pain from the incision sites. I was unable to work for a month while I recovered. My speech was slow at times, but otherwise, I did not appear to suffer any brain damage. (Although, some of my loved ones may beg to differ.) I noticed after I returned to work my mouth worked slower than my brain, especially in stressful situations, like arguing in court. Mostly though, my brain and heart returned to normal.

My shoulder was a different story. The doctor sent me back to physical therapy to see what kind of mobility I could recover. After a month, the physical therapist informed me I was making no progress. I would just have to decide whether I was willing to risk undergoing surgery again. Uh, let me think…for about two seconds…uh, no! I still could not lift my arm in the air and was in unbearable pain. One day I cried out to God telling Him, "Thank you for keeping me alive. I appreciate it, but I cannot live like this. This pain is unbearable. I want to be able to do this," as I tried to lift my arm. Only this time my arm went straight up in the air, just like that. The impingement released and the pain subsided. He healed me. I have been very careful with my shoulder ever since as I can get occasional discomfort but it has never frozen up on me again. Thank you, God!

40.

After my recovery, I went on a cruise to Alaska with a Christian singles group. My trip was amazing! The beauty of the glaciers and the fiords brought healing to my soul. I rode a train ride through the Rocky Mountains and even flew on a seaplane back into the fiords. I heard an unforgettable comment from a tour guide regarding Alaska. She was talking about the high ratio of men to women in the area saying, "The odds are good, but the goods are odd." Haha. I met a guy on the cruise who I liked and had several dates with him afterward. It was nothing serious but I think it helped to open my mind to dating again.

One paralegal I worked with was in a tumultuous situation and she needed to move. I let her and her son move in with me. I loved her. And she was a great paralegal! However, in doing so, I brought the stressful, chaotic world of family law right into my living room. I tried to help her with her case against her son's father but it seemed to be never-ending. I took her on a cruise to Mexico with me, as a little getaway and a reward for her hard work. While we were gone, her son's dad was stalking around my place and messed with her car. It was too close for comfort. We had to part ways. She moved out.

I also had to make a change in my workplace. Some issues with the other paralegal forced me to come to a decision. I needed to move on. So I gave the ladies my notice and moved my office into the Bank of America building in Valencia. I rented a lovely office there and was surrounded by other family law attorneys. I had built my practice so I never had a lack of work, or maybe such is just the nature of family law. In any event, I was doing well financially and was fairly happy in spite of the stress of the workplace.

I also was enjoying The Vineyard. As it happened, the church's pastor retired and we had a new guy come in. I watched the attendance fall over time from about 700 people to about 30. I guess the old establishment didn't care for the new regime. It was sad to see but I still loved this place. This new pastor announced one day that we were going to team up with a group from Overcomer's Church in North Hills for a prayer ministry called "Healing Rooms." We would train with them for a year and then start our own Healing Rooms in Valencia. That sounded exciting to me. I loved to pray for people, so I volunteered to be part of the team.

The premise of the Healing Rooms was there were different teams of two or three people who would pray for 'clients' privately in a room for up to 20 minutes. When the client came in they would fill out an information sheet, including their prayer request. The sheet would be given to the team prior to the client entering the room. The team prayed over the sheet before reading it, to see if God would reveal anything specific to pray for that person. Then the client came in and the team prayed for them. We met every Friday night at Overcomer's Church.

I met a man at the Healing Rooms named Perry. Often the director paired us up on a team together. I watched him minister to people and thought he was a nice guy. Sometimes people from our prayer team went out to eat after we finished for the evening. It seemed like Perry and I ended up sitting next to each other quite often and one day he asked me to go out with him. He seemed nice so I agreed to go to dinner with him. We had Italian food. No surprise there. On our next date, we attended a church gathering together. Then I ended it. This guy was far too serious. I could see where this was going. If I continued dating him, I would end up married again. I did not want that to happen! So, I told him I only wanted to be friends.

I did not want to marry a fourth time. I didn't feel I had anything left within me to give to any man. The Bible describes marriage as "two becoming one flesh." Well, my heart was fractured by three disastrous marriages. It was in splinters. How do you bond with yet another person? I was unwilling to try again. I was not willing to do what it takes to be in that kind of relationship.

Karen, the director of the Healing Rooms began a subtle campaign with me. "Linda," she told me, "He is a nice guy. You need to look at this." I declined. She persisted, "What if we do group activities together with him? Get to know him."

One night I prayed over a prayer request in the room with my team. When I put my hand on the sheet I saw a big brick of shining gold and heard, "This next person has a heart like this." I was not prone to seeing visions. Sometimes I heard things. Sometimes I just sensed things about people. But this night I saw a brick of gold as clear as could be. And who walked into the room but Perry. Sometimes the staff would receive prayer after we finished with the clients but I was not expecting the client with the heart of gold to be Perry.

Karen asked me to go away for the weekend with her, her husband, Jim, and Perry. We would stay at a condo in Del Mar and I would have my own room. That way, she explained, I could spend time with Perry and get to know him better. I probably would have declined but for the "heart of gold" experience.

We spent the entire day on Saturday sitting in the living room talking. I never changed out of my pajamas and never put on any make-up. I thought that might deter him, but no. That night we walked on the beach and he told me he loved me. I became rather upset and asked him, "Please don't say that anymore."

I joined a women's group at the Vineyard. At the first meeting, the leader explained that we were all there for a reason. She had prayed diligently about whom to invite. I looked around and noticed all the other women were married but me. The leader looked at me and started humming the wedding march. *"What?"*

So I started dating Perry. It seemed God had an agenda for me. After dating for about six months, I had a gut-level feeling he would propose. I went away for a week to a Vineyard Worship Conference. I wanted to hear from God. And hear from Him I did. He said, "Marry him." Psalm 32 jumped out at me several times during the conference, the part that says, "Do not be like the horse or the mule which have no understanding but must be led by the bit and bridle or they will not come to you." Okay. I can't say I understood everything that was going on in my life or that my fears had changed much, but if God said it, I would trust Him. I had already seen where my own choices had led me and I wasn't impressed. If Perry was God's choice for me, so be it. Shortly after, Perry proposed and I said yes.

Perry and I got married six months later on December 4, 2004. We married at Overcomer's Church with both of our pastors performing the ceremony. I did not sleep much the night before and it showed. My stomach was in knots, screaming, *"What are you doing?"* When you have been married multiple times, the divorces may get easier, the wedding ceremonies do not. As you walk down the aisle, perhaps wearing white or maybe off-white, something inside questions, *"Wait, haven't I done this before?"*

It was mostly our church friends and close family who attended the ceremony so I was shocked when I walked into the reception hall and saw almost 200 people there. A lot of Perry's family had chosen to skip the church part. All the people cheered and clapped. I felt like Cinderella! I hadn't wanted a large ceremony but Perry had been alone for thirteen years and he had a large family. So we began our new life. And I gained two more stepchildren, Rocco and Angela.

Perry and I both sold our condos and purchased a home in Valencia, which is where we spent our honeymoon night. When we arrived, we discovered our friends had been there and had tossed fresh flowers petals from the front door back into the bedroom. It was just lovely.

The next day we caught a plane for Calgary, the first stop in our month-long honeymoon in Canada. We drove through Banff up to Lake Louise in the Rocky Mountains. I had called ahead to our hotel, the Fairmont Chateau, to ask if they would put a bottle of champagne in our room since we were newlyweds. This was one of two places on our trip where we planned to splurge. Much to my surprise, when we checked in they gave us an upgrade to a room that cost $750 a night. It was on a private floor with a private chef. It was the most luxurious room I have ever slept in! The lake was frozen solid. As a result, I had my first and only experience of walking on water.

Next, we flew to Montreal and spent time in the old city. We attended a performance of Handel's Messiah in the glorious St. Patrick's Basilica, a dream come true. Remember, I was a choirgirl. We drove from there to Old Quebec City and stayed at the Chateau Frontenac, our other splurge. I was hoping for a similar upgrade but oh well, it was a grand experience anyway. The hotel is like a fortress surrounded by the city walls. And Old Quebec City is a quaint European village. They speak French there and even if they also speak English they will pretend they don't. We enjoyed the amazing food, the snow, and the eccentric people.

From there we drove south, or Sud as they say in that part of Canada, to Vineland, just south of Toronto. We planned to spend Christmas with Perry's family and flew our children there to be with us (three out of four children, anyway). For a wonderful two weeks, we visited the surrounding area, Niagara Falls, Hamilton, Balls Falls and the CN Tower in Toronto. We ate the most wonderful Italian home cooking and enjoyed family time. Although I will admit, I was a little alarmed when Perry's mother said to me, "Linda, I hope you can be patient with him." *"Oh no, what have I done?"*

We had some issues with the local hotel where we stayed in Vineland, the Days Inn. Perry's brother had arranged for a special rate since we planned to stay there for two weeks. Maybe they got irritated when I complained about the blood on my blanket in my room. They changed it for me but then tried to kick us out for New Year's Eve, even though our room was still booked. Or maybe they just wanted the extra money they could get for the room on that special night. The Fairmont, it was not. Whatever. We left and found a nice bed-and-breakfast and didn't return.

My children had their first experience with an authentic Italian family dinner. They learned you do not chow down on the pasta because it is only the first course. There is so much more to come.

41.

So began my latest journey, being married to yet another man. I would like to say this will be a fairytale ending but that's just not the nature of life. Relationships are hard work and I came from a pretty damaged place. Perry, although kindhearted, is a type-A personality. We had some strong cultural differences, especially in the kitchen. I wasn't looking to be a Sous Chef. I didn't enjoy being told how big to chop the tomatoes. So I backed out of the kitchen and left it to him. My "Linda's Kitchen" sign that my brother Steve made for me went into the garage.

With Perry, I learned the difference between personality and character. His personality could drive me crazy. Things such as calling me from across the house and expecting me to come running and interrupting my every sentence, I found frustrating. Communication was difficult. Would I ever be able to finish a thought? It's hard to believe you are important to someone when they don't listen to you. And the fact that I explained to him hundreds of times how those things made me feel, yet saw no long-term change, was a continual challenge. They seem like little things and, in fact, the issues were small compared to others I have experienced, but they were still hurtful.

On the other hand, Perry's character was beyond reproach. He was a hard worker, unlike Rick. Unlike Greg, he loved my children. He was faithful, unlike Tom. And he always loved me, which I'm sure wasn't always easy. He showed tremendous patience when I struggled. So what is truly important in life?

Before we married Perry told me he had no problem with me quitting work, in fact, he said he would prefer it. I didn't intend to quit but at least his comment showed me he wasn't looking for a cash cow. (Although he seemed rather disappointed when I sold my classic green Jaguar and bought a Camry) After we married though, there was an incident that changed everything. My favorite judge (not) ordered me to supervise a property exchange between my client and her husband… on a Sunday. I did not feel comfortable being there alone with my client 's husband as their relationship was volatile, so I asked Perry to come with me. When he saw the tension and bitterness that I dealt with he was shocked. He told me later, "You have suffered through three divorces. How can you ever heal when you deal with this stuff every day?" Good point.

I was ready to listen at this point. I was so tired of dealing with people filled with hate and anger and determined to inflict damage. People who once loved each other enough to make babies together were now intent on the other's destruction. Perry was right. It was hard for me to heal surrounded by turmoil all the time. I went to UCLA and took an extension course in Estate Planning. I thought that area of the law, preparing Wills and Trusts, would be more low-key. I found out though, siblings could fight just as vehemently as any divorcing couple ever did. It's always about the money! I did not quit my practice immediately. I began a transition, which took several years, and even then, I would continue to take family law cases selectively, usually by referral from friends, former clients or family.

One of the most heartbreaking cases I ever worked on came to me by way of a friend of Perry's. He needed a guardianship of his granddaughter because his daughter, recently released from prison, had been arrested and would likely go back to prison on a parole violation. She was a druggie and the granddaughter just a baby. So I appeared in court and got a temporary guardianship for him. As it turned out, the daughter did not go back to prison and she fought the guardianship.

94

Over the next six months, we had to go back to court several times since the judge wanted to give the daughter time to get her act together. I understood that the judge was trying to be compassionate when he gave possession of the baby back to her, but she had never fully complied with her drug-testing program. We had even submitted proof she had tampered with her drug tests. It was a deadly mistake. You cannot imagine the devastation when only two weeks after the mom got her baby back I received a phone call. The baby was dead! Yes, this is hard work.

42.

In 2005, Perry and I took a trip to Italy. We flew into Rome and spent the next two weeks on a tour that took us from Rome all the way north into Switzerland, Lake Como, south again to Florence, Pisa, Siena, Verona, Pompeii, Sorrento, Positano, Capri, the Amalfi Coast, back north to Venice and back to Rome. What a wonderful tour! We saw so many famous sites, such as the Coliseum, the Spanish Steps, Trevi Fountain, the Vatican, and the Sistine Chapel in Rome. It surprised me to see the Hand Of God painting by Michael Angelo, which I loved so much, was only one of many frescos on the ceiling of the Sistine Chapel. I thought it covered the entire ceiling. We saw the Statue of David in Florence, the dismembered, mummified head of St. Catherine in Siena, and the balcony of Romeo and Juliet in Verona. I sailed in the canals of Venice and was careful not to fall in. The tour guide warned us about the polluted waters. He told us we would have to go to the hospital and get "the shot" if we fell in the water. I did not want to go get "the shot."

We bought tiny silver spoons in Switzerland for our future grandchildren. I enjoyed German beer and knockwurst in Lake Maggiore. I did my best to avoid the Nigerian vendors in Pisa. As I looked upon the ruins in Pompeii, I wondered what it must have been like to be there when it all went down. I rode the funicular in Capri and thought it was very touristy. Perry and I walked the narrow roads in Positano and marveled at the beauty. I took it all in and loved every minute.

I also learned so much about Italian culture. For example, the Italians don't do lines. If you want your espresso, you must push your way to the front. And with Italians, when they are all talking loudly, all at the same time, they really are not fighting and they really can hear each other. Good to know, even though it is a little stressful to my sensitivities.

Next, we rented a car in Rome and tried to find our way back out of the maze to the Autostrada, the highway. (All roads **do** lead to Rome, so much so you can't get out!) My next lesson about the Italian culture was even though they drive like maniacs, they don't seem to have many accidents. And the Autogrills, the roadside cafes, have tasty food but you must elbow your way to the counter to order. We drove south to the Abruzzo area, to Perry's hometown of Gagliano. His mother and aunt were visiting there as well so we spent the next two weeks with them. Gagliano is a small town up in the more mountainous and cooler area of Italy. It is lovely. We visited the surrounding areas, such as L'Aquila and Castelvecchio, which were later hit by an enormous earthquake. And we visited my favorite town of Sulmona, a quaint village town nearby. It is famous for its confetti and I bought a pretty linen tablecloth there. We watched Italy's victory of the World Cup on a large screen the people had set up in the piazza, the town square of Gagliano. The crowd's excitement was contagious as caravans of cars drove from town to town, hooping and hollering out the car windows and beeping their horns. And the authentic Italian food was amazing.

43.

In 2007, we moved to Acton. I loved our little home on Avenida Capella in Valencia but Perry kept talking about wanting more land. He asked me to at least go out and take a look. I didn't want to move again. I had been moving my entire life. But we found a beautiful two-story home out there, so I agreed to move once more.

The following year Kelli graduated from Samra University with a degree in alternative medicine. She had worked hard for years to accomplish this, working full time and going to school in the evening and weekends. Our new home had a lovely pool with a waterfall so we had a party for her at our house. She invited friends from all over and everyone had a good time. I did get perturbed at Perry for micromanaging all the details and bossing me around. And my back was hurting, so I went outside and sat by the pool.

Then I got irritated with Kelli's stepmother, Eva when she came out and made some comments about me sitting down. I thought it rude to boss me around in my own house. I guess that's why I didn't notice Kelli's friends refilling my wine glass more frequently than I was used to. Kelli laughed the next morning, "the only one who drank too much at my party was my mom." Oops, sorry, Kelli! Such a good reminder: watch out Butterfly! Alcohol is always laying in wait for you. It's in your genes. You can enjoy a glass of wine or even two, but you must always be mindful!

As a reward for her hard work, I took Kelli on a trip to Scotland and Ireland to visit our roots. We flew into Dublin and from there we began our tour of the "forty shades of green," as Kelli called it. Dublin is a lovely city on the mouth of the River Liffey. We strolled along the river, enjoying the multi-colored buildings. We also tasted the original flavor of Guinness. I've never been much of a beer drinker but this beer is wonderful! Someone told me it does not travel well. Even in Scotland, it tastes different. So I decided I must have one every day while in Ireland.

We visited Trinity College where I purchased a book on the origins of the Layton name. From there we took the bus to Kildare and visited a beautiful racehorse-breeding farm. Then, on to the famous Blarney Castle where Kelli kissed the Blarney Stone. After seeing the upside down and backward position required to do the feat, I declined. Plus, I was a little grossed out by the thought of all those lips on the stone. We drove the magnificent Ring of Kerry on our way up to Waterford where we toured the Waterford Crystal factory. Kelli bought me a lovely crystal cross. Next stop was Londonderry, also known as Derry. They still did not take tour groups to Belfast in those days, but in Derry we saw some remnants of the Northern Ireland conflict. The Derry walls were covered with graffiti and many pictures of the war. I will never forget a statue I saw in the park. It was a man and child going one direction with the wife and another child going the other, with their backs to each other. I'm not sure but I think this might have represented families being broken apart.

From Derry, we drove to the Giant's Causeway on the shore of Northern Ireland. It is an amazing area of volcanic hexagonal columns, which is now a World Heritage site. According to Irish myth, a giant built the Causeway to get to his lover on the other side in

Scotland. It is spectacular! We spent quite some time hiking down to the rocks and out around the sea.

From there we took a ferry across the sea to Scotland and continued our tour through Glasgow, along the western coast of Scotland, overlooking the Firth of Clyde and up to Loch Lomond. I was a little disappointed with Glasgow. I had been looking forward to seeing it since my Nana was born there but it looked like just a big, old city. I wasn't disappointed we didn't spend much time there. As we continued north we passed through an area known as Glencoe. It has the most breathtaking, dramatic landscape! I felt like I arrived on another planet. From there we moved on to Fort William and received a history lesson on the defeat of the Jacobite army. (Think Outlander) Hearing the stories and viewing the memorial stones of the clan massacre, I wanted to renounce any English blood I might have running through my veins. We visited Loch Ness on our way up to Inverness and Culloden. Kelli bought a stuffed Nessie and took an adorable picture of herself with Nessie, positioned so it appeared Nessie was swimming in the lake out the window of the bus. So cute!

Deep into the Scottish Highlands, there is a large farm where we experienced a sheepherding demonstration. We watched as a group of border collies, following their owner's direction, surrounded a herd of sheep. With their circling and barking, they moved the herd from one area to another. However, one sheep escaped and got away. It ran off into the far pasture followed by one lone dog trying to bring it back into the fold. That sheep finally stopped and just stood its ground, glaring at the dog as if daring it to do something. This scene reminded me of the parable in the Bible that describes Jesus leaving the ninety-nine to go after the one lost sheep. I wondered if most lost sheep end up in that position because they acted as this sheep had, running away in rebellion. I could relate to that sheep, both in its flight and in its rebellion and was reminded, I have to learn to stay this time. I have to stay close to God and with Perry.

Someone once said that when we stand before the Lord in heaven, His question to us will be, "Did you learn how to love?" I want to be able to say, "Yes, Lord!" That means I must learn how to set aside the foolish romantic notions young girls seem to grow up with. My love cannot be based on worldly lust. I want to stop chasing silly illusions and learn how to love unconditionally, the way God loves us. He is the One who never leaves the lost one behind.

We finished our time in Scotland in Edinburgh, touring the castle, which sits high upon Castle Rock. I had learned of a Scottish delicacy on one of Perry's TV cooking shows, a deep-fried Mars bar, and I was determined to find one. Find one I did, at the last shop I looked in, on the last day. Yummy!

44.

In 2008, after our move to Acton, Perry and I attended a church in Lancaster. It was a small church but I liked it because they worshipped in song for at least an hour every Sunday. I loved the music. It made me feel closer to God to worship for such a long time. This church was my first real introduction to the prophetic movement. I had experienced "prophecy" before but these people were deeply involved with it. It was also a crash course in "end times" theology. Some of it seemed a little weird but I wanted to learn.

We hadn't been there long when the pastor announced that a prophet would be visiting the church from India. "He is amazing and you will be so blessed," he said. I was a little surprised when the prophet arrived to see he wore a long yellow robe, long hair and beard and looked like a Hindu priest, which he may have been at one time. He spent most of the time talking about a conference he was holding in Israel and encouraging everyone to attend. I never had any desire to go to Israel but listening to this man, I felt a deep desire to experience this land. So did Perry. So we signed up for the trip, which was to take place in two months.

The conference was quite interesting. It took place on the Mount of Olives, in a tent. The view was spectacular, overlooking the old city of Jerusalem. But the tent was like a sauna! It was June and the weather was warm, with little circulation inside. It was a challenge to stay awake at times. I remember little in the way of details of the content of the conference. But I remember a lot of talk about the end times and how we have to prepare. (Think, "Winter is Coming," from the Game of Thrones) And we had to take our shoes off before entering because this was "holy ground."

The prophet from India told us repeatedly we would see the "Lion of Judah", who is Jesus, at this conference. He would show himself to us. I did not understand what that meant but certainly wanted to experience it. The leader mentioned the conference was being televised in several countries and people had reported seeing the lion on their television screens. I found that interesting but wanted to see the lion for myself. I didn't want to just hear about it. Maybe I'm just a skeptic. I had trouble with some of what I heard about the "end times" and how we were to prepare ourselves for it. The prophet told us we are much closer to the end than we realize. He also gave some unfamiliar teaching about some Christians being appointed to stay behind after the Rapture. I never heard or read anything about that anywhere! But I enjoyed the conference for the most part and learned a lot.

On the fifth and last day of the conference, we took communion. I was disappointed I hadn't seen the lion but then there were others who hadn't either. I knelt in front of my metal folding chair to pray and take the bread and wine. All of a sudden, I had a vision of the Lion of Judah! It was as if a veil was pulled back behind my eyelids and there He was. He wasn't the image I had imagined, not a ferocious, roaring lion. Rather he looked almost like a cross between a lion and a lamb, smiling at me with eyes of love, as I have never seen before. His eyes were like liquid LOVE. The vision only lasted about five seconds and then it disappeared. Funny how the two times I've seen manifestations of Jesus have happened while taking communion. It was such an awesome experience, one that would stay with me as a wedge of faith in my heart.

I had to take pause one night in the hotel dining room. After giving a fairly large donation to the Indian prophet's ministry that day, he approached me in the dining room and told the female leader I was talking to, "Take good care of her, she's part of the family now." I had to wonder if the timing of that encounter was a coincidence since a couple of hundred people attended the conference. Why would he pick me out? I had my doubts. But then, I did see the Lion of Judah, didn't I! Why is everything always a mixed bag? It's confusing.

After the conference, we began a five-day tour of Israel. We visited the Garden of Gethsemane, the Kidron Valley, The Church of the Nativity, the Pool of Bethesda, the

Garden Tomb, and the Western Wall. I sensed the strong presence of God at Gethsemane and then again at the Wall, which surprised me, as I was not expecting anything special to happen there. When I placed my hand on the Wall to pray, I felt such power surge through me. Was it the power of God or the power of all the thousands of prayers offered there? My knees suddenly buckled and I could hardly stand.

From Jerusalem, we went to the Sea of Galilee where we visited the place purported to be the site of the Sermon on the Mount. We saw the "Jesus Boat", a relic from the time of Jesus. We traveled to Capernaum to the ruins of a temple where it is said Jesus taught. (I believe that is true as I again sensed His strong presence there.) The house of Peter is also located nearby. Next, Perry and I got baptized in the Jordan River. We both had already been baptized but we were in the place where Jesus was baptized so why not?

The last stop was Mount Carmel, where Elijah killed the prophets of Baal. I thought we would have a meeting in the chapel there but instead the Indian prophet hiked down the mountain through the bush and bramble, expecting everyone to follow him. As I walked down the mountain in my sandals, I complained in my head, *"I wish they had told us we were going to do this, I would have at least worn tennis shoes. What about the older people who can't do this hike?"* Then, I heard that still, small voice, "Linda, do you want to do this or do you want to go back and sit in the bus?" I decided to zip it. We walked about halfway down the mountain and then stopped to worship and pray. On my way, I noticed cattle roaming loose about the area. They stood and stared at us as if saying, "What are you doing here?" It was a little eerie.

The view was incredible. The Valley of Megiddo was directly below us. It is described in the Book of Revelation as the location of the Battle of Armageddon. I could not help but imagine this lush, beautiful valley below filled with bloodshed and bodies.

From there we drove to the airport in Tel Aviv. We were exhausted after such a long day and did not board our plane until after midnight. For some reason, they stopped Perry and me at the gate and took our passports away. I thought, *"What is their problem? Security is tight in Israel but we had no issue when we entered the country, why now?"*

After detaining us for about five tense minutes, the staff came back and told us they had upgraded our tickets to first class. They gave no explanation. I never learned the reason but those recliner chairs could not have been more welcome. I was a little sad for the others in our group as we left them for the front of the plane, but not that sad. We had a layover in New York, where we parted ways with our group and flew to Canada to visit Perry's mom.

45.

In 2009, Perry approached me with a proposal. We had some dear friends, about my age, who had five adopted children, all under the age of twelve. They were struggling financially and having some difficulties where they lived. Perry asked me if I had ever considered renting out our house to them and buying another house in Lancaster. That way, we could help them and we would be closer to the church, where we were now pretty involved. I hadn't. I loved my beautiful home. Moving again was the last thing on my mind. But… I felt bad for our friends and wanted to help. We had been talking about buying a rental property in Lancaster. I just didn't plan to live in it. Be it guilt or compassion, I know not, I relented and agreed to rent them our home. So, we ended up buying a fixer-upper ranch-style house in Lancaster on ¾ of an acre. It had five bedrooms so it would make a good end-times house if it came to that. The house needed a lot of remodeling, most of which we tried to do before we moved in.

Around the same time, we were scheduled to leave for another trip to Israel. But the remodeling work was delayed so long we ended up moving in the day before we left. None of the work was finished in the house so we had to stuff most of our things into the back room and sleep there before leaving for the airport in the morning. Welcome to Lancaster.

Overall, I still enjoyed the church. I loved the worship. That was the big draw for me. I thought the pastor was a little eccentric, kind what I imagined John the Baptist would have been like. I could imagine him wearing a camel hair garment and eating wild locust and honey. But I wasn't looking for any heroes these days anyway. I had one disturbing experience though. The pastor called for a forty-day fast. The Indian prophet had told him if the church fasted and prayed for forty days, God would show up and do signs and wonders. The idea excited me. I hadn't done a forty-day fast since I was a new believer. I couldn't fast all food because of blood sugar issues. (Thank you, Perry, for all that yummy pasta and pizza!) So I just restricted the type and amount of food I ate. I attended early morning prayer at the church every day. I tried my best to seek God. I loved it. I even had an inspiring dream. I dreamt I went to the airport to fly out of the country. After arriving at the airport I discovered I had forgotten my passport and did not have enough time to go home and get it. I would miss out on my trip. I interpreted this dream to mean I was not spiritually prepared for my second trip to Israel. So I put my whole heart and soul into the fast and sincerely prayed. I was also very careful to pack my passport when I left for Israel.

During the fast, the pastor had a volunteer running around with a camera, ready to record all the signs and wonders that God would do. It never happened. At the end of the fast, the pastor scolded us saying we had failed. If we had done it right, God would have shown up. I had done my best so I had a real problem with that. It was very discouraging! We can't manipulate God to do what we want or think He should do, even through prayer and fasting. God is God. We are not.

Around this time we had friends come and stay with us. They had some financial difficulties and needed a place to stay. It wasn't a convenient time to have houseguests as we were in the middle of remodeling our kitchen, but they needed help. We had set up our refrigerator, a hot plate and a microwave in the dining room along with our dishes. When all four of us were in the dining room trying to get a meal, there was barely enough room to turn around. We washed dishes in the bathroom sink. What a mess!

This man saw himself as a father figure to many women, including me. I sort of accepted it but will admit I was a little reserved. I tend to be a little cautious anyway but I wasn't sure I needed another father. Besides, it was a struggle to watch his wife go out to work every day while he stayed home and had his afternoon nap. I'm a little sensitive that way.

103

One day, after the fasting incident at the church, I was in our prayer room by myself, having some quiet time. "Daddy" came in uninvited and informed me that the reason I had problems with my blood sugar was because of depression and anger. Hmm, well maybe. He told me he always thought any issues in my marriage were Perry's fault but now he could see Perry did not stand a chance with me. I was not a happy camper.

To make matters worse, Perry came home from work that day and decided he didn't like the way they laid the flooring in the kitchen and proceeded to tear it all up. Our remodel had been going on for a long time. Between the issues at the church, "Daddy's" oh so encouraging advice and the turmoil in my house, I thought I would explode. I told Perry I wanted to go away by myself and stay until the flooring in the kitchen was finished. He agreed. So I drove to the Santa Cruz Mountains to the same Catholic retreat where I had stayed so many years ago.

I spent a wonderful week in a cabin up there by myself. The theme for this trip was "But God". I cannot say I had lightning bolts from heaven on this trip. This time I just relaxed into the peace of God. No matter what anyone thought of me, no matter what anyone said about me, no matter the turmoil in my life, my God loves me. And that's what matters. It is the bottom line to everything. Song of my heart: "*You Are For Me*" by Kari Jobe.

46.

The second conference in Israel was more of the same, how to get ready for the end times as the Bride of Christ. One day during the conference, the Indian prophet told us not to go to sleep that night until at least 2:00 am, if at all. He told us to pray and ask God if anything in our heart displeased Him. Losing sleep wasn't my favorite thing, but I stayed up and prayed for a while. It didn't take long to get an answer. Rather loudly I heard, "Pride!" Who me? I don't think of myself as a prideful person, but then who does? Who can recognize their own pride? I now think of this experience as the highlight of the conference and something I would consider in my heart for a long time.

On the post-conference tour, we traveled to most of the same places we visited on the first trip, with a few exceptions. We stood across the street from the Knesset, Israel's parliament, and prayed for the country. Then we went up into the West Bank and saw the so-called Israeli "settlements", which were actually well-established neighborhoods with actual homes, markets, and schools.

We drove to Masada, which is an ancient fortress in the Judean Desert overlooking the Dead Sea that was built around 30 BC. There is a choice of taking a cable car up to the top or climbing 700 steps. I took the cable car. A group of us sat in the ruins of King Herod's Palace praying together and talking about the passage in Ezekiel 37, which speaks of God's breath on the Valley of the Dry Bones. It was awesome! I later learned that this passage was found in the rocks during an excavation of the area.

The next stop was the Qumran Caves where the Dead Sea Scrolls were found. We made an unscheduled stop in En Gedi where King David hid from Saul. En Gedi is now an oasis near the Dead Sea and is kept as a natural reserve. Our tour guide told us, if we were lucky, we could see goats up in the mountains. But they weren't up there when we arrived. Instead, as we drove in the entryway, animals were lining the road on both sides as if they had come to greet us. It was a strange and wonderful place, which left me in awe.

47.

In 2010, I made my third and last trip to Israel. Perry did not go this time since he had to work. So I went with the rest of the group from the church. We traveled to Egypt first and attended several days of the conference there. Our trip took place about six weeks before the Arab Spring occurred and you could cut the tension in the air with a knife.

Strange things happened there. One lady somehow fell into a fountain in the hotel's lobby. She was okay but the Bible she carried got soaked. Another lady freaked out when she came looking for our group and couldn't find us. She convinced herself that Arabs had abducted the entire group. I enjoyed seeing the Pyramids. They are an incredible sight but the spiritual atmosphere is dark and I did not feel particularly safe anywhere in Egypt. It was so intense that a leader in our little church group called a meeting for us to pray for the safety of all.

We drove by bus from Cairo to the Red Sea where we spent the night before crossing over to Israel. The flies were horrible! That night in my room, I had a fly that buzzed me every time I was about to fall asleep. The thing would dive-bomb me. Finally, I covered my face with my blanket leaving only a small opening to breathe. Sure enough, just as I was almost asleep, the thing came into my breathing hole! *Demonic flies! Get me out of here!"*

Leaving for Israel the next day, we had to go through Egyptian customs on one side of a long building, then through Israeli customs on the other side. We had a long line and it took hours. I struggled with my luggage since Perry wasn't there to help me and I was not paying attention to much else. I certainly was not feeling very spiritual. When I emerged on the other side, the Israeli side, I noticed all the flies disappeared. The oppressive heat lifted and a fresh breeze was blowing. All of a sudden I felt the strong, distinctive presence of Jesus, as if He stood there with His arms wide open, saying, "Welcome home." It was so overwhelming! I had to go sit down on a small block wall, and with tears in my eyes, take it all in. Just then a lady who had been walking in front of me came back over and asked me, "Did you feel that?" She had the same experience. I later learned many people had the same experience. It was another wonderful memory to tuck away in my heart and remember in times of trouble.

I remember little of the rest of the conference except the Indian prophet stated several times there were some pastors there "in sin" and if they didn't repent bad things would happen to them. Ok, that sounds all too familiar. It made me uncomfortable. The after-conference tour was pretty much as it had been the previous two times and I was ready to go home.

On the way home I had an interesting layover in Germany. As our carry-on bags were going through the scanner, the German security officer meticulously checked each and every bag, resulting in a very slow process. We became a little anxious about catching our flight in time. He found something he didn't like in the bag of a man in front of me and took him off to a private room. In his place, he left a young guy who clearly didn't know what he was doing. When this young guy searched my bag he found a bag of mud, which I had taken from the Dead Sea. This is how the conversation went:

Guard: What is this?

Me: It's mud.

Guard: Mud?

Me: Yes, it is mud from the Dead Sea.

Guard: Mud. Mud?

Me: Yes. It's good for your skin.

Guard: Mmm, mud. I don't think I can let you take this.

Me (with pleading eyes): Please, it's harmless.

(Meanwhile, people behind me are getting antsy. Guard looks around for a superior to inquire further but sees no one.)

Guard: Oh 'Fawk' it (expletive with a German accent). Go on.

Shocked at his language but happy to keep my mud, I grabbed my bag and ran for the plane.

One other thing happened on this trip to Israel that affected me deeply. God told me that Rick, my first husband and the father of my children did not have long to live. He had been battling Non-Hodgkin's Lymphoma for years but so far had been winning the battle. Rick and I were not on speaking terms at that point. He had written a book earlier that year to which I took great offense. He had asked me to read it and sent me chapters, one by one. As I started reading, I initially took offense because I thought he made me sound like a crazy person. He claimed I had a nervous breakdown and seriously needed help. He also disclosed personal things about my family and me. These things were not his story to tell. But I read on. By the middle of his book, I became outraged. He claimed our marriage ended because I had an affair, that I had been seeing someone for nine months. It just wasn't true. Rick had always tended to embellish his stories. Let's just say he was familiar with creative license. I guess that's why he referred to his book as being "semi-autobiographical." He claimed he wrote this book for his future grandchildren. If that were the case, why would he tell them such a thing about their grandmother? I also felt that even if this had been true, (which it wasn't) some things that happen between a man and wife should remain private even if they don't stay together. There are some things I will never tell anyone about him! In my opinion, he not only lied about me but also violated my privacy.

Unfortunately, the situation came to a head on Drew's birthday. We were all supposed to meet for dinner at a steakhouse. I could hardly speak, I was so angry. I didn't know how I would even look at Rick. Perry had to stop the car along the way and pray for me. I don't think I had ever been so angry with Rick, even during all we suffered through in our marriage. In retrospect, I should have just gone home. I think I ruined Drew's birthday for him. Sorry, Drew!

Rick wanted to get together for coffee and discuss the situation but I just wasn't ready. I told him I didn't want to read anymore. I emailed him the changes I wanted him to make in the book and explained the reasons. We argued for a while, via email, but he promised he would make the changes I asked for. I wish I had known then his time was so short. I would have been more willing to sit down and truly have a conversation with him.

After I returned from Israel, Rick went into the hospital for the last time. I knew this was the end for him because of my experience in Israel and somehow all of my anger toward him disappeared. I cried out to God on his behalf, begging God, "Please do not let him leave this earth without You!"

I was surprised at the depth of my emotion considering how angry I had been with him. Four days before he passed away, he called me from the hospital. His voice was so weak it was almost impossible to understand what he was saying, however, I heard him say he was sorry and he loved me. I told him, "Don't worry about it, everything's in the past now." And I told him I loved him too. Kelli later told me he seemed almost giddy the rest of the day. I called his wife a little later and asked her if he wanted me to come but she said, "No, he just wanted to tell you he is sorry." Maybe he didn't want me to see him in that condition, or perhaps he was hoping I would come. He probably would have come to me if the situation were reversed. But I will never know. I decided to respect their privacy. I don't know if anything changed in his relationship to God or lack of it, but I believe there was forgiveness between us. I am thankful that God prepared me for his death and that I could release him and let him be free.

48.

That year I encountered another life-changing development. Perry had to go out on disability because of a bad back. Not only was he off work for some time but also the condition caused him to take an early retirement. I couldn't complain, of course, the man was in pain. I couldn't help but wonder though, "*Why? No matter who I am with they always stop working.*" I don't think I would have dismantled my law practice if I had known he was going to retire so young. Oh well, good thing I am not terribly materialistic.

The next few years at the little church in Lancaster became increasingly difficult for me. I still loved the worship, but it seemed like every week I would show up to receive my weekly rebuke. The pastor viewed himself as an exhorter but it didn't feel like mere exhortation when you were on the receiving end. It felt like guilt and condemnation. I felt hopeless as if nothing I could do was good enough. The messages were always long, condemning and full of fire and brimstone. Each week, I anxiously waited for him to finish so I could go home.

The pastor described on numerous occasions how God had told him to start this church in Lancaster. He said he argued with God, saying, "There are already many churches there." "But God wanted there to be a church where His presence would be," he said. The inference was that God is not in any of the other churches in Lancaster. The same attitude was prevalent throughout the church. We are better than others. We are what's happening. It bothered me.

I acted as a leader of a small women's prayer group by this time, known as a cell group. We had our meetings on Wednesday nights. The church also had prayer meetings on Thursday nights and Friday nights and Saturday nights and Sunday mornings before service. The pastor expected people to attend a majority of these meetings, especially cell group leaders. It was all-consuming and all the non-stop activity all too familiar.

The stars of the prayer meetings were those who prayed loud and long. Since that was not my style I don't think Pastor considered me a "prayer warrior." This became abundantly clear to me during one of our annual conferences. I was manning a book sales table and several of the prayer warriors were assigned to work with me. A messenger came running in to tell them, "You need to go to the prayer room immediately. Pastor wants someone in there who actually knows how to pray." Not only did it confirm my suspicion of his attitude but left me shorthanded on my table. That was not very important though, I'm sure.

On a more serious note, I began to question, more and more, this whole business of the prophets. The pastor had a stable of them who would come several times a year to tell us what God was saying and doing. On one occasion, one of the visiting prophets called me out of the crowd and told me "God wants to prosper you financially. There is some kind of inheritance waiting but something has held it up and it is large. There has been a problem with the paperwork but God is going to fix it." After the meeting, I approached the prophet and told him I thought that would be wonderful but I didn't have any idea what inheritance it could be. He immediately said, "Oh well, it may just be a spiritual inheritance. It may just be spiritual." I didn't argue, but I thought, *"That's not what you said."*

It also seemed these prophets talked an awful lot about this or that angel or dead saint being in the room and they were telling them this thing or that. This smacked of mysticism, which deeply bothered me, especially the dead saint part. The Bible is clear about there being a gulf between here and there. We can't talk to dead people and they can't talk to us. Besides, who could either prove or disprove such a claim?

There seemed to be an attitude of elitism toward these guys who heard from the angels and the dead saints. Anyone not on their level just hadn't arrived. The pastor respected these men and didn't seem to want to listen to anyone else. I also had a hard time with the push toward rituals, such as "you need to get up at 3:00 in the morning and pray. That's when God is available. If you don't pray then, you've missed it." These kinds of things spoke of a "works" mentality, which contradicted the basis of the grace and mercy of God as I had learned and experienced it. Like you must earn God's blessing.

There also was a lot of division within the body of the church. Rumors went around about this person or that person. Certain people gave "Words from God" to other people such as, "God told me you are supposed to marry this person," and, "God told me you are not supposed to marry that person." All kinds of weirdness! And it caused a lot of damage in people's lives. It was all very confusing.

We were friends with a couple in the church who lived in Idaho and also part-time in Lancaster. They started a new church in Boise and invited us to join them. We made several trips to Boise and stayed with them to check it out. Then, we learned one prophet had prophesied we would move there and be part of their work. We seriously considered it at one point but it never worked out. I sure liked Boise though. Our friendship with the couple kind of fizzled after it became clear we were not going to move, which was sad.

In 2012, I decided to leave this church. It was a difficult decision because Perry and I had many close friends there. And Perry didn't want to leave. I don't think he was aware of the things I saw or maybe they just didn't bother him. I tried my best to "eat the fish and spit out the bones," but things came to a head when the Indian prophet came for the church's annual conference in Lancaster. The man finished his last speaking session at the church by telling all the parents in the room to lay hands on their children and dedicate them to be martyrs. He did not tell them to dedicate their children to the Lord, but to be martyrs! I got sick to my stomach. I hung my head between my knees and used all my restraint to keep from screaming. Afterward, I told Perry, "I am never coming here again. Don't try to make me." I understand there are occasions that children have and will die as martyrs but I cannot accept the idea of dedicating them to such a fate. How is that any different from what radical terrorists do? And how must those children feel to have their parents lay hands upon them and publically dedicate them to die? After the prophet finished speaking, the pastor got up and said, "Well, we have just heard from God." I did not think so.

111

We tried to meet with the pastor to explain to him why we were leaving. We believed it was the right thing to do. The pastor was always too busy. He finally told me in an email, "You have already made up your mind anyway." He obviously didn't want to hear anything we had to say so we let it go. Leaving our friends at the church hurt. No one seemed interested in continuing a relationship with us after we left. If you are not with us you're against us, I guess. Maybe we would contaminate them? So once again I walked away from my entire social structure. I became isolated again.

I write about this experience entirely from the viewpoint of my own perspective. I know in my heart the people at this church love God. I do not judge or condemn them. However, their approach to practicing Christianity just did not work for me in the long run. It left me hurting and confused. I needed to move on.

49.

I spent the next two years processing what had happened at that church. It was a process similar to the one I experienced when I left Buddhism. I searched my mind, my heart, and my soul, asking, "What do I believe about God and what beliefs were put there by others? Who is God? What is He really like? Is all of this really just a fairytale? Is God good or is God angry? Where is the balance between grace and judgment? What does it all mean?"

For the first time since becoming a believer in 1989, I stopped going to church, something I had never imagined doing. Oh, Perry and I visited some different churches, but I just didn't find any church where I wanted to be. They were either superficial or manipulative. I'm sure I was super-critical at that point. I needed to sort some things out.

So I prayed. And I read books, a lot of books. I read about the grace of God. I read about the futility of performance-based Christianity. I remembered all the times that God manifested Himself to me. I thought about all of my experiences with Him, how they were all so warm and loving. And I knew that He is real. I knew that I could never walk away from Him.

I read my Bible. This book was dead to me before I became a believer. Before joining Buddhism, I signed up for training in Transcendental Meditation. They encouraged reading the holy book of whatever religion you believed in. So I tried reading the Bible even though I knew nothing about Christianity. I couldn't do it. It meant nothing to me. But, after opening my heart to Him, this book came to life. I don't understand everything in it, especially in the Old Testament and probably never will while I am still walking on this earth. But I have come to believe it is His Word. It has come alive by His Spirit. Without the Holy Spirit, it appears to be just nonsense. His Word guides me and instructs me. Scriptures jump off the page to encourage me. It tells me who God is. It shines a light on my path, my journey. And during this time of deep soul-searching, it was my anchor.

I remembered when I was a leader in the Buddhist organization. I attended a special lunch with President Ikeda, the leader of the international Sokagakkai. All the members adored this man. As I said earlier, they sang songs to him and about him. They flocked to him if they were in his vicinity, so much so he required bodyguards, one of whom was Rick. Whatever he said was the final word. He was Sensei, the master. I sat across the table from this man at a restaurant in Malibu. This was an event attended only by the 'great white hopes of the next generation', by invitation only. It was quite an honor. However, as I sat there I found I had nothing to say to him. I had no questions for him. I felt nothing. I knew he was not my master.

Now, in the same way, I came to realize my heart belongs to no pastor, no teacher, and no prophet. All men are flawed. They all have their own agenda. Some men want money. Some men want power and/or sex. The Bible says all men are right in their own eyes. It's true, even of me. Some men have great motives and intentions but they are still only men and we all fail at times.

During this time of apparent "falling away," God helped me to renew my mind and my faith in Him. I renewed my trust that He is for me. He will always be there for me and will never leave me or forsake me. This is the relationship I always longed for, His love. No earthly man can ever be that for me and no earthly man can ever take that from me. I will not follow a man. I will only follow THE MAN. Jesus came to earth in the flesh, died and was resurrected and in doing so eliminated the need for any intermediary. That's not to say there aren't men I admire and respect. There certainly are. I may always struggle with cynicism but I would rather be cynical than deceived by false teachings or manipulative people ever again! I will also always be careful with mysticism. There is such a thing as true prophecy, which comes from the Holy Spirit of God. I know supernatural things happen. I don't want to throw the baby out with the bathwater, but in my experience with God, the true life-changing encounters have not been initiated by me and not by a man. God has always initiated them. I just need to stay open. I need to seek Him. My job is to keep my eyes on God.

50.

In May 2012, Perry and I made another trip to Italy. His nephew got married and rented a villa in Florence for the family. About fifteen of us stayed in this beautiful villa. I call this "the Paolone Family Vacation." It is quite an experience being in a house full of Paolones for an extended period. They are a loud, passionate lot. Almost every discussion ends up in a boisterous disagreement, usually over food or because someone wasn't listening while they were interrupting. They are the only people I know who can engage in a heated argument over whether it's okay to use garlic powder instead of fresh garlic. It can become a challenging overload for me. But there is also a lot of love in the big Italian family.

We started the vacation by taking a train from Rome to Florence. Then we attempted a four-car caravan from the train station to the villa. It was a crazy idea in Italian traffic. Perry's brother, Alex and his wife, Tracey, got lost in the process. We stopped at a park along the route and waited for them to catch up. Five hours later we gave up and drove to the villa. Perry's mom was distraught. She had his passport so Alex and Tracey could not even check into a hotel since the passport is a requirement in Italy. He also did not have his cell phone. And it seems there are two villas known by the same name. One was not at all close by. So if Alex stopped to ask directions, it was entirely possible he would end up driving a long way in the wrong direction, which is exactly what happened.

Later that evening we all left for dinner at a local restaurant. Alex and Tracey still had not arrived. The mood was dark. We were all concerned. Halfway through the meal, we received a phone call. Alex and Tracey were at a bar about a half-mile down the road having a great time with the locals. And so it goes.

The wedding was lovely. They held the ceremony in the backyard of the villa, overlooking Florence. I worried that we would burn Florence down with all the fire lanterns we sent up into the sky that night, but all went well.

After our stay in the villa, we took a train to Venice with Perry's other brother, Tony and his wife, Linda. She became know as Senior since her name was Linda Paolone before me. I became know as Junior, even though I am older. I like being a Junior. We did the usual touring in Venice and then took a boat to Burano, known for its tapestry and colored houses. We also went to Murano, known for its glassworks. Unfortunately, I managed to knock over a glass bowl with my shopping bag while in a store. That cost us a couple of hundred dollars, which almost spoiled my day.

From there the four of us flew to London, where we spent another four days. I loved London. There was so much to see. Our hotel was within walking distance of the Tower of London Bridge. We took a boat ride on the River Thames. We rented a car and drove to see my 'family castle', the Oxburgh Hall. In doing my family genealogy a few years before, I found a family line that traced back to the year 1030. The family line consisted of lots of lords and ladies, which is why the records were intact, I suppose. Anyway, I discovered they owned this castle, located about an hour north of London that is now maintained by the government and therefore open to the public. I just had to see it. I was tempted to walk in and announce, "I'm home!" It was a relief to know not all my ancestors were drunken alcoholics.

51.

In June 2012, I received some amazing news. I'm going to be a grandmother! Drew's former girlfriend, Melinda, had attended Rick's memorial service and one thing led to another. They got back together after not seeing each other for ten years. Even more amazing news arrived a few days later when Drew called from the emergency room. He had taken Melinda there because she started bleeding and they thought she might be having a miscarriage. Instead, the doctor told them there were two gestational sacs. Twins! Drew was so shocked and excited he said he couldn't even find his way out of the hospital parking lot! I had almost given up on having grandchildren, now there would be two. Actually, there would be three because Perry's daughter, Angela, was also pregnant. I also inherited Melinda's 23-year-old son, so that makes four. (And Angela later gave birth to another boy.) My family is growing!

This development ended our discussion of moving to Boise. I didn't think it would at first because I loved Boise, loved our Boise friends and wanted to be part of starting their church. Perry and I had even looked for property there. I was in Boise when we got the news that the ultrasound indicated it would be two girls. I realized then I simply could not leave my future grandchildren. Maybe that is why it hadn't worked out. After it became apparent we would not be moving to Boise, I did not feel as welcome with our friends there and over time we just stopped communicating. Perry was hurt by this development. I just accepted it. Maybe I had just experienced so much disappointment with people I could not allow myself to feel it this time. I don't know.

(Note to self: 2019, Boise friends reached out to us. We have had several visits and a wonderful reunion. Sometimes misunderstanding can cause much hurt. Honest communication can go a long way in avoiding this type of thing!)

Avery and Madison arrived on March 1, 2013, five weeks premature. Melinda had been in the hospital for five weeks already, trying to keep them in. They were already big girls though. Avery weighed 6 lbs. 6 oz. and Madison weighed 5 lbs. 3 oz. and both were healthy. They only stayed in the NICU for the afternoon. Avery was a blondie, like me. Maddie looked like her Mama. Oh, the joy! What precious gifts these girls are!

Melinda's mother was already deceased and she had no other family to help her so I stepped up to the plate and tried to be there for her. She became another daughter to me. She returned to work three days a week when the girls were six weeks old. I drove down from Lancaster on Wednesday afternoons and stayed until Saturday mornings. I loved being with the babies, although some days were stressful being there alone with them. Sometimes I would go back home so exhausted I couldn't even talk. But I would not trade this time with them for all the money in the world. Good thing I had already retired!

In May, my brother Steve passed away. He had been battling a rare form of stomach cancer, known as GIST, Gastrointestinal Stromal Tumor, for many years and had several surgeries, the first of which took half of his stomach. I watched as he struggled. He took an oral chemotherapy medication, Gleevec, which made him very sick. Yet he continued to work, even though sometimes he had to go outside and throw up in the bushes. He fought hard for years. Finally, it spread to his liver. He asked his wife to take him to the emergency room on Tuesday. I visited him in the hospital on Friday after receiving the news. There was nothing more they could do for him. He sat up in bed, somber but alert. The doctor sent him home that day and ordered hospice care for him. I went to see him at his house the next day and was shocked to find him unconscious, out of it. I asked, "What happened here?" He died the following Tuesday. Maybe he was just tired of fighting. Or perhaps he was spared any more suffering.

Many young people from his workplace came to say goodbye to Steve before he passed. I sat and listened to their stories, surprised to learn how he had impacted so many of them. They thanked him for his encouragement and friendship. He was like a father and big brother to many of them. I had no idea.

I was with him when his moment came. Unlike my dad, Steve was struggling. I told him, "Don't worry Steve, we will all be okay here. Just go. If you see Jesus stretching out his arms to you, run to Him." Immediately, I felt his spirit leave his body and he was gone.

I helped Steve's wife and son make arrangements for his memorial service. Not being religious they did not want a religious ceremony. So we asked the hospice chaplain if he would perform the ceremony, keeping it simple. He agreed but later got offended when the family wanted to play the song, "Red Solo Cup," which Steve loved. He had promised the family he would be there for them if they had difficulty speaking at the service. Steve's daughter-in-law did, in fact, break down and turned around searching for the chaplain to help her. He was gone. Left early. I guess he didn't want to be there when they played Red Solo Cup. That made me sad. I thought he missed an opportunity to be the hands and feet of Jesus. No wonder Jesus hated the religious spirit of the Pharisees. Jesus came for the lost. He was always a friend to sinners.

After his memorial service, a friend and co-worker of Steve's posted a song on Facebook in tribute to my brother, *"Temple of The King"* by Ritchie Blackmore. I had never heard this song and fell in love with it. I pray Steve had this experience. He had been mad at God for many years because he lost his son, Chris, when he was only 23 years old. Chris came home sick from work one day and died in the middle of the night. He had diabetes. No one even knew he had it. Steve told me, "It's not that I don't believe in God anymore. I just don't like Him very much right now." Before he died, I asked Steve if he had fixed his relationship with God. He assured me he had. I hope he and Chris had a great reunion.

52.

Perry had a part-time wife for about eighteen months. I didn't want to give up my time with the babies so we sold the house in Lancaster and moved closer to the family. I can't say I was upset to leave Lancaster, even though I loved the house. I hated the area and after leaving the church there, Lancaster held nothing for me. We rented a house in Chatsworth for about six months while we looked for a house to buy. I lived only five minutes away from the kids so I enjoyed going home at night.

We purchased a house in Simi Valley and I told Perry, "That's it. I never want to move again!" This time made 43 moves in my lifetime! And that's assuming my parents only lived in one place during the first five years of my life, which is not likely. Financially this house was more of a struggle for us. Our expenses were four times what they had been in Lancaster. But we were close to the family instead of being out in the godforsaken desert. And in my mind, being near family is much more important than having a lot of money. I guess we all have our priorities.

So here I am back in Simi again. Corriganville is gone. The town burned down many years ago and the area is now a park. The Old Santa Susana Pass is still there with its rocky landscape, which I love so much. And on the top of the Pass is a cross overlooking the valley. Halfway down the Pass is the Church at Rocky Peak. Perry and I decided to give it a try.

I liked this church from the first service I attended. The pastor introduced himself as "one of the pastors", which to me was an indication of his character, a person of humility rather than control. He is well educated and understands Hebrew and Greek, which adds so much in the way of context in his teaching of scripture. His messages were challenging but balanced and practical, not condemning. They took an offering but never pushed for money. I liked the worship. So, I decided to stay awhile. We joined a small group and make new friends. I am still there. It has become a place I enjoy, a place of healing. We started serving in different ministries but in a balanced way that did not require our every waking moment. I am happy to be part of a community again. I am also happy to be in a place where I do not feel manipulated or coerced. You don't have to speak 'Christian-ese' or pretend to be something you are not. Instead, the pastor puts a strong emphasis on being authentic and radically honest. And I believe I am hearing the truth in this place. Favorite songs: *"No Longer Slaves,"* by Bethel Music, *"Alive"* and *"Bird Set Free,"* by Sia, and *"New Wine"* and *"So Will I,"* by Hillsong.

I continued to be with the girls three days a week and loved watching them grow and develop. Maddie has some sensory processing issues and has therefore been challenged in some ways. She started having meltdowns at eighteen months old. Loud noises were difficult for her and she had trouble dealing with frustration. But she had lots of help learning to cope and deal with her emotions. Sweet baby. Avery was always precocious, always everywhere and into everything. They are both beautiful and smart. They brought such joy to my life. I recently cut back my time with them to one day a week. It is getting harder for me to keep up with them. I get tired more easily, struggle with back pain and I'm probably not always as patient as I should be. They need more at this point, someone who can keep them busy going to parks and such. As they continue to grow, they will need me less and less. That's the natural course of life. It makes me sad but I understand. And I am so grateful for the time I had with them. I love them both with all my heart and will continue to pray for them always.

Angela's boys, Anthony and Nicky, are also near and dear to my heart. I love their tender hearts and will continue to pray for them as well.

53.

It is Memorial Day 2018. I woke up at 6:30 a.m. to what I thought was a message from my brother, Larry. However, when I called his number his wife, Diane, answered. In tears, she said, "He's gone!" Larry always joked about the day that he would have his heart attack, as if he owned it and had it all planned out. I think that was the way he wanted to go. And I believe he knew it was coming.

A week before he died, Larry called to see if Perry and I would like to go to a Dodger game. He had season tickets but wouldn't be able to go on this particular night because he had to get up early the next day for a court appearance. Perry is not really into sports and I hadn't been to a Dodger game in approximately forty-five years, but for some reason we accepted. It was Cory Seegar bobblehead night and Larry asked if we would mind getting one for him. When we arrived, he gave us a grand tour of the stadium, via cell phone, telling us where to go, what to eat and introducing us to the stadium attendants in his seating area.

Since Larry was so kind as to give us his tickets, we decided to make a special trip out to Acton and give him his bobblehead. We took him to lunch and spent a wonderful afternoon visiting and sharing stories. That was the Saturday before he died. I am so thankful for that time with him!

Larry's death brought a flurry of expected work my way. I needed to help Diane go through all of his files and deal with his current cases. I was amazed to find notes in different files stating, "If a lawyer is needed for this case, call…." Diane found the key to the mailbox, which was located a mile down the road. It had a note on it that identified the proper key. That was interesting because Diane had never collected the mail in all the years they lived in this rural area.

Larry and I had talked about getting together to visit some of the houses where we lived in our youth. We even set a date but he finished by making the strangest comment, "I don't know, that date may be too late for you."

For all of these reasons, I believe he knew he would die soon. Looking back on that afternoon we spent with him though, he seemed so happy and in perfect peace. I miss my brother.

54.

I was 70 years old when I started writing this. It has been two years and I am now 72 years old, still trying to finish it. I already outlived my mom by nine years. No one knows how much time they have left. It could be one more day or another twenty years. These past two years have been a time of reflection. Looking back on my youth, I realize I was pretty hard on my mom. Yes, she was difficult to live with. She screamed a lot. She was drunk most of the time. As a teenager, I never stopped to wonder why she was that way. What did she go through as a child? I came to understand that there were surely many reasons for her issues. I'm sure she suffered and self-medicated as a result. I have also come to realize that I was probably not a piece of cake to live with. I no doubt added to her suffering as a rebellious teenager. She also had to watch me reject the God that she had come to love and become immersed in Buddhism. That could not have been easy. I know now how she prayed for me and that she loved me. I look forward to seeing her again someday.

A few people told me I must harbor resentment toward my dad. After all, he did nothing to stop my mother's behavior. He drank along with her. He didn't stop her tirades and didn't protect me. So I searched my heart to see if I could find any resentment inside. I can't. I loved him. Every female wants to remain a "Daddy's girl." It never occurred to me until recently that some accusations my mom made against my dad could have been true. Maybe he did push her down the stairs when she was pregnant with me. Perhaps he did have a girlfriend in Italy when he was away in World War II. Maybe he did have an affair when we lived in Lakeview Terrace. And maybe he did hit her where it wouldn't show. He never shared much about his life. Did he have something to hide? If so, my mom was an abused woman. That would explain some of her drinking problems. I will never know. I wish I had more compassion for my mom when I was younger. But then, most young people don't. They are wrapped up in their own lives and are usually pretty self-centered. Only a lifetime of experience, of hurt and struggle, bring a person to a place of a little wisdom and compassion. A life lived brings perspective. I may not have learned to cook or clean as a young girl and I didn't learn how to be a mother. I certainly didn't learn how to communicate or be in a relationship. But I witnessed both my mom and my dad turn their life around, love God, and serve the poor. What great examples they were!

My children are my greatest treasure. I haven't always made great decisions in my life. But my kids were always in my heart. I always believed I was serving their best interests even while making huge mistakes. As they grew into adulthood, I watched them struggle and also make choices that broke my heart. Nothing pierces a mother's heart more than seeing her children suffer. But such is the nature of life. We all have our own journey and must find our own way. So as long as I am here on this earth, I will continue to pray for them. I pray they would know and love God with all their heart. I pray they would know God's perfect love for them… intimately.

As I mentioned, I forgave Rick. Forgiveness was not so easy for me toward Greg and Tom. It is much easier for me to just numb it all out and forget. Move on. However, I found anger and bitterness just hide inside me and affect everything, my perspective, my joy and especially my ability to give and receive love. I learned forgiveness is letting go. It is not making excuses. If behavior were excusable, it would not need any forgiveness. It is wishing for a person's highest good. So I pray for them too. I pray they find all God has for them. And I now understand forgiveness is a supernatural work. We are all broken people. If I hadn't been so broken myself, I'm sure I would have handled those relationships differently. I need forgiveness as well.

Thank God for Perry! You could call me a reluctant bride. But Perry has loved me through it all. He has patiently showered me with love even when I gave him little in return. His love has brought tremendous healing to my life. Now I understand why God said, "Marry him." Thank you, sweet man!

I know I probably sounded pretty critical of some people in the Christian community. I don't mean to judge. It's just been so hard for me to find the real meaning of this life. At the risk of sounding preachy, I want to share some thoughts. I don't like religion. Religion kills! I don't like legalistic dogma and ritual, adding man-made rules to God's Word and I don't want to be a Pharisee, i.e. I don't want to be self-righteous. I want to set aside my preconceived ideas about God, life and other people. For me, Christianity is only about loving God. It is about learning how to be in a real relationship with Him every day of my life. Proverbs says every man is right in his own eyes. The truth of that statement is reflected everywhere, in religion, in politics, education… everywhere. And it seems in order for a person to be right, he must make people who don't agree with him wrong. It makes us feel superior, I guess. There is real freedom in learning to say, "I don't know." So I no longer think I must have an opinion on everything.

I love the Jesus I encountered. I know only too well the wretchedness of my own life. The Buddhist concept that I could ever become my own god, "Buddha," is a joke to me now. Life has shown me what I can and cannot accomplish based on my own abilities. I decided as a troubled teenager to pull myself up by my bootstraps and become a survivor. That determination only took me so far. Ultimately, I found myself unable to change my own anger when left to my own devices. Mostly, I hardened my heart, put on my mask and kept walking. Those were my survival skills. I need the Holy Spirit to work love in me. I love how Jesus loves. His grace, mercy and unconditional love are the truth I cherish. He is the one who leaves the ninety-nine to go after that one lost sheep, even if it got lost due to its own rebellion. He never leaves the one behind. I have tried to learn to love that way, although I'm not very good at it yet. As of today I still have time to learn.

DIDI, UNCLE RALPH, LARRY AND ME. LARRY LOOKS THRILLED!

MOM LOOKS HAPPY TOO!

LOOK AT MY DARK HAIR!

KINDERGARTEN

LINDA AT KNOTT'S BERRY FARM

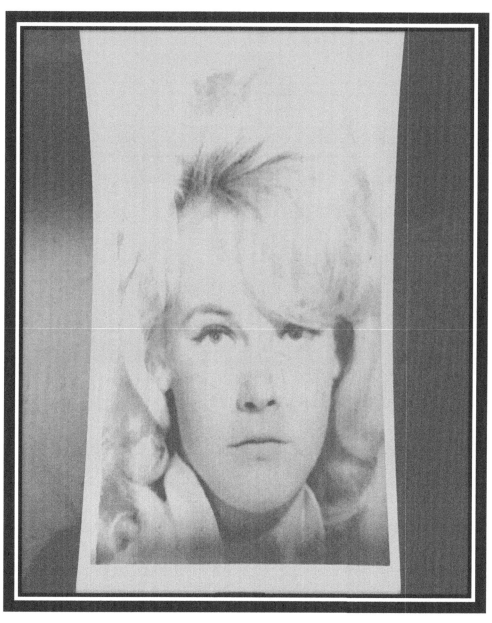

WELCOME TO HIGH SCHOOL

HANDS IN THE AIR, CRASH!

DELAFINA, BILLY THE KID'S GIRLFRIEND

(RICK IN THE BACKGROUND)

THEY KILLED BILLY!

AM I MY MOTHER'S DAUGHTER?

TATTERED AND TORN DELAFINA

A RARE, SWEET SMILE FROM LINDA

MY BABIES!

LITTLE CUTIES!

KRISSY, KELLI, KEITH, DREW, AND LITTLE LINDA

GOOD TIMES!

WORSHIP!

STEVE, ME, AND LARRY

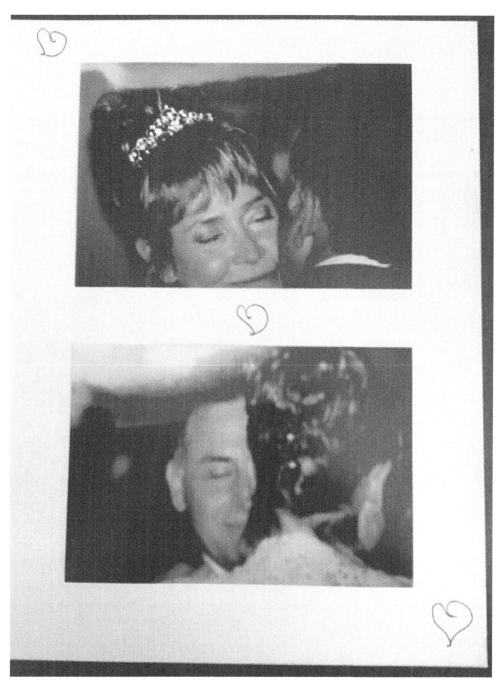

AND THEN THERE WAS PERRY

AND BEAUTIFUL ANGELA

WELCOME TO THE PAOLONE FAMILY
ANGELA, PERRY AND ROCCO

MY BOY, ALL GROWN UP

AND MY GIRL TOO! IS SHE HER MOTHER'S DAUGHTER?

AVERY AND MADISON, MY LOVES

OH SUCH BIG GIRLS

AND THE BOYS, PAPA, ANTHONY AND NICKY

MELINDA, AVERY AND MADDIE, HAPPY MOTHER'S DAY

Made in the USA
Coppell, TX
07 September 2020